Confessions
a Black Acade

# Confessions of a Black Academic

*A Memoir*

ALVIN J. SCHEXNIDER

McFarland & Company, Inc., Publishers

*Jefferson, North Carolina*

LIBRARY OF CONGRESS CATALOGUING-IN-PUBLICATION DATA

Names: Schexnider, Alvin J., author.
Title: Confessions of a Black academic : a memoir / Alvin J. Schexnider.
Description: Jefferson, North Carolina : McFarland & Company, Inc.,
    Publishers, 2024. | Includes bibliographical references and index.
Identifiers: LCCN 2024020169 | ISBN 9781476693378
    (paperback : acid free paper) ∞
    ISBN  9781476652054 (ebook)
Subjects: LCSH: Schexnider, Alvin J. | African Americans in higher education. |
    African Americans—Education (Higher) | Discrimination in higher education—
    United States. | Historically Black colleges and universities. | African American
    college teachers—Biography. | African American college presidents—Biography. |
    BISAC: BIOGRAPHY & AUTOBIOGRAPHY / Personal Memoirs | SOCIAL
    SCIENCE / Ethnic Studies / American / African American & Black Studies
Classification: LCC LA2317.S334 A3 2024 | DDC 378.1/982996073—dc23/
    eng/20240521
LC record available at https://lccn.loc.gov/2024020169

BRITISH LIBRARY CATALOGUING DATA ARE AVAILABLE

**ISBN (print) 978-1-4766-9337-8**
**ISBN (ebook) 978-1-4766-5205-4**

Front cover image: Alvin J. Schexnider, 2013 (Winston-Salem State University)

Printed in the United States of America

*McFarland & Company, Inc., Publishers*
  *Box 611, Jefferson, North Carolina 28640*
   *www.mcfarlandpub.com*

# Contents

# Acknowledgments

Over the course of my career I have collected a lot of memorabilia, some dating to my childhood. Because I have kept a lot of it I qualify unequivocally as a packrat. One example is the telegram my mother sent to my dad announcing my birth. At the time he was serving in the segregated Army so it bears a Paris, France, postmark. I have also kept identification cards including one issued by Queens College in 1964! These mementos are usually but not always accompanied by fond remembrances but equally important, they are invaluable in storytelling and for that I am grateful.

In writing this memoir I have lots to remind me that I am indebted to many individuals. Many but not all are fellow travelers in higher education. Some were colleagues and friends and others were people I met and collaborated in the course of a career that spanned more than four decades. My academic colleagues were critical to my professional development and my ability to navigate the shoals of race and racism in every aspect of my life. I owe them a debt I can never repay. Our deep conversations shaped my views and actions and they have influenced what I have written here and elsewhere. I alone, however, bear responsibility for this memoir.

Over the years I have had the good fortune of being able to rely on four exceptional individuals who provided administrative and clerical support: Dorothy Giannini, Teresa Harnish, Nira Holton and Annette Montgomery. Dorothy (Dottie) Giannini passed several years ago but I kept in touch with her to the end and I remain in regular contact with Teresa and Nira. I discovered Annette toward the end of my career. She prepared this entire manuscript and continues to provide exceptional support.

# Acknowledgments

Several friends read all or most of the draft memoir and provided invaluable comments and suggestions, all of which led to substantial improvements to the final product. I am particularly grateful to Christopher Brooks, Daryl Dance, Jackson T. Wright, Jr., and Governor L. Douglas Wilder. James Walke, a mentee, was a huge help in collecting, analyzing and interpreting data on racial representation among faculty at selected universities. Hugh Perry, a friend of more than fifty years and a fellow political scientist, also read and critiqued the entire manuscript. Hugh has been both a beacon and a sounding board throughout my career. I have learned much from his wise counsel and critical thinking on a wide range of topics both personal and professional.

I would also like to recognize many colleagues who were helpful at various stages in bringing this project to fruition. Some contributed to expanding the horizons of my research or pointing me in certain directions. Others were helpful in providing critiques or engaging me in thoughtful discussions of certain topics germane to race and higher education. I am particularly indebted to Wayne Davis for his expertise on all things pertaining to computers and information technology. I am also grateful to the following individuals: Terricita Sass, Tod Massa, King Davis, Napoleon Peoples, Rodner Wright, Yuka Hibben, Nakeina Douglass-Glenn, Tyrone Baines, Willie Pearson, Jr., Emma Perry, Richard Bunce, Edwin Blanks, Aashir Nasim, RaVonda Dalton-Rann, Verna Holloman, Jack Ezzell, Jr., Leroy Gross and Susan Gooden.

I am grateful to my friend and fellow traveler Vann Newkirk for connecting me to McFarland. My editors, Dré Person and Layla Milholen, have been wonderful to work with and enormously helpful throughout the entire process

Last but not least, I wish to thank my family, specifically my wife Virginia and our children Alvin and Elena, for their steadfast support and unconditional love throughout my career. It is likely that I am among the last generation of academic nomads whose careers have been marked by moving from one university to another in pursuit of better opportunities but which invariably may have been perceived as a search for the Holy Grail. The moves were difficult for all of us but especially for our children and for that I bear full responsibility and guilt for the challenges they posed. Withal, it has been an unforgettable journey that has been enriching, purposeful and I hope of value to those I was honored to serve and work with. As well, I am indebted to my family, friends and colleagues who made it all possible.

# Preface

On September 14, 1970, I was discharged from the United States Army after completing a tour of duty in Phu Bai, Vietnam. Fourteen days later, I started graduate school majoring in political science at Northwestern University in Evanston, Illinois. In between, I had just enough time to visit my mother in Lake Charles, Louisiana; drop off my duffle bag; and rush to Evanston to find a place to live, register for classes and start a new life in unfamiliar surroundings.

Thus began an academic career that was unplanned and one that no one in my family had embarked on. I was new to the area, and as I was to discover, Northwestern was adjusting to me and several other Black students as well. In 1970, the civil rights movement was entering a new phase that stressed Black pride and economic empowerment. Anti-war sentiment, although still strong, was declining as President Richard Nixon sought to end the Vietnam War and bring the troops home.

As a graduate student adjusting to a new life, I tried to make sense of what I was experiencing. Competing demands for my attention in the classroom did not allow for much thinking about what lay ahead as an academician, so I simply plowed ahead. Except for what I observed among the faculty, I had no idea what life in the academy was like. In fact, my primary motivation to enter graduate school was to get out of Vietnam as quickly as possible. The military's early-out program that enabled soldiers, sailors and marines to shorten tours of duty by much as ninety days facilitated my desire for an early exit.

Truth be told, I had no idea where I was headed. By law, my old job as a personnel trainee at Owens-Illinois in Toledo, Ohio, was kept open for my return. Instead, I opted for graduate school even though I was unclear about the future. Once I had a Ph.D. in hand, what was I to do? The logical answer was an academic career and that is how I started.

My first job was in 1973, as assistant professor of political science at Southern University in Baton Rouge, Louisiana, approximately 150 miles from Lake Charles where I grew up. My first visit to a college campus was at Southern in 1962. I was there twice that year, in the winter to participate in a statewide academic competition, and in the summer to attend Bayou Boys State, a leadership development program sponsored by the American Legion. I returned to the Southern campus in summer 1963 as a Bayou Boys State counselor.

The campus of Southern University sits on a bluff of the Mississippi River, a naturally beautiful setting befitting its mission, history and culture. I had hoped to stay at Southern a long time but the desire to conduct scholarly research was simply not possible with a four-course teaching load. So, after one year, I moved on.

My next appointment was as an assistant professor of political science at Syracuse University. The Maxwell School of Citizenship and Public Affairs is arguably among Syracuse University's best known programs. The department of political science is housed in Maxwell, but did not enjoy the acclaim of public administration. My years at Syracuse were unpleasant for the most part, mainly because of the racism I found there. After a few months I learned that the dean of the Maxwell School, Alan K. (Scotty) Campbell, leaned heavily on the department to hire me and the faculty resented it. The department was composed of white males with the exception of a lone female, and I believe the faculty wished to keep it that way. When Scotty Campbell left to join the administration of President Jimmy Carter in 1977, I lost a major supporter. There were a few Black faculty at Syracuse at the time, however; I befriended some with whom I have remained in touch. Because of them, I was able to weather some very difficult circumstances.

My brief years at Syracuse University taught me a lot about race and the academy. I was indeed a neophyte learning by trial and error.

The Maxwell School had a handful of Black faculty: Otey Scruggs in history, Harlan London in human development, Louise Taylor in regional and urban planning, and Ruth Gossett, who later died in Africa while on sabbatical, on the social work faculty.

Charles V. Willie, vice president for student affairs at Syracuse, shared with me during my campus visit that he was leaving to accept a faculty appointment on the Graduate School of Education at Harvard University. Having spent his entire academic career at Syracuse from graduate student in sociology, earning tenure and advancing to full professor, he knew the university and the academy well. With the tact and diplomacy of one well-heeled in the art of scholarly dialog, Dr. Willie tried to warn me what to expect. I did not always heed his wise counsel but I have never forgotten it. Rather than being direct and labeling it racism, Willie told me to beware of how easy it is for a Black academic to be taken for granted. I interpreted this as at least one example of what Ralph Ellison described in *Invisible Man*. Willie's advice was on target.

A constant goal throughout my career has been striving to ensure that I was neither taken for granted nor becoming invisible. On more than one occasion at a conference or in a meeting, I have made a comment or an observation that was simply ignored as though I was not there, a not so subtle reminder of Ellison's *Invisible Man*. In the same meeting, a White person would make the same comment, drawing immediate reaction. After this happened a few times early in my career I learned to express myself in such a way that I would not be ignored but this too caused offense and stirred comments that I was too direct. Throughout my career, this has been a challenge because subtlety has never been my strong suit. Yes, I tend to be impatient and direct but I know of no other way. My Gemini horoscope offers a defense: "You tend to be as direct and forthcoming as possible. Sometimes people misread your approach and don't understand how your wit and humor play into the moment." I totally agree, yet I cannot deny that these character traits probably affected my career in a fashion not always conducive to advancement.

I make no apologies for who I am and how I have comported myself. In the seventh decade of my life unequivocally, there has been progress yet race continues to insert itself in every aspect of society. American higher education suffers from this malady as society writ large. The prospect of a nation where minorities will become the majority within two decades offers the possibility of a diminution of racial prejudice, or so one hopes, but I doubt it. Racism is deeply embedded in the fabric of American society. In their minds White male superiority is tantamount to religion; it will not go gently into that good night. But neither will African Americans who must be reminded from time to time of the wisdom of the great abolitionist Frederick Douglass: "There can be no progress without struggle; there never was and there never will."

# CHAPTER ONE

# 1708

Early in my career, I saw a short training video entitled, "*You Are What You Were When*." The video struck a chord with me since basically, it was a story about how one's view of the world is shaped by the times we grow up in, and how experiences at a certain stage influence beliefs and expectations. For example, people who experienced poverty or the loss of money or property during the Great Depression may be motivated to save or even hoard, so as not to relive that hardship again.

Well, I grew up in the segregated South and easily recall Colored and White water fountains and unpaved streets in Black neighborhoods. I attended Sacred Heart Catholic School from kindergarten through the twelfth grade. Although taught by White nuns and priests, it too, was segregated. Many of our books were used and came from the local White public schools. So yes, my outlook on life was shaped by those experiences.

1708 Winterhalter Street, Lake Charles, Louisiana, was my refuge from the harsh realities of racism from the time I was born until I left for college. It was where my parents stressed hard work, honesty, independence and responsibility. My mother detested lying of any type. My dad placed a premium on planning, encouraging us to "make the necessary preparations" for whatever goals we had. My parents believed that doing just enough to get by was unacceptable. My father never used profanity, but if he referred to someone or a situation as "trifling" it might as well have been. The last thing I ever wanted to be called was trifling.

The lessons and expectations we were taught at home were reinforced at school and vice versa. Every six weeks we received our report cards that our parents had to sign. These reports were dispensed by the pastor of Sacred Heart. During most of my elementary school years that would have been Father Clement Roach who always ended his presentation with the admonition "work hard, play hard and pray hard." More than half a century later, these words still resonate strongly, richly affirming how deeply they have influenced my life.

Neither in high school nor college did I ever contemplate an academic career. My high school and college years were sandwiched between the civil rights movement and the Vietnam War. The countless murders of civil rights workers during the 1960s, when I was in high school, particularly the brutal slaughter of Andrew Goodman, James Chaney, and Michael Schwerner in 1964, are forever etched in my memory. Sixteen years later, the symbolism of Ronald Reagan launching his bid for the presidency in Philadelphia, Mississippi, where the atrocities occurred, did not escape me. Instead, it was a stark reminder that even in 1980, I still felt the pang of that atrocity, and it alerted me that Reagan's avowed conservatism was currying favor with racial sentiments embedded in the party of Lincoln.

My original career goal was to join the ranks of executives in the private sector. During college job opportunities were expanding in the federal government and the private sector. Martin Luther King, Jr., and other civil rights leaders realized that passing legislation to secure basic civil rights was necessary, but not sufficient for full participation in society. This is how Dr. Martin Luther King summed up the situation:

> The Negro today is not struggling for some abstract, vague rights, but for concrete and prompt improvement in his way of life. What will it profit him to be able to send his children to an integrated school, if the family income is insufficient to buy them school clothes? What will he gain by being permitted to move to an integrated neighborhood, if he cannot afford to do so because he is unemployed or has a low-paying job with no future?[1]

The draft and subsequent duty in Vietnam led to graduate study in political science and a career in academia. Race has been a constant companion throughout, a shared reality with many. Being Black in American society is a heavy burden, particularly for competent, self-confident Black men. Far too many have succumbed to taunts designed to draw a perception of seething anger. Frankly, I have not always carried this burden well, and I am quite aware of when, where and how. There are no apologies to be made and no scores to settle. Suffice it to say, that my early upbringing, my college years and military service were key factors in shaping my leadership style, and my unwavering commitment to fighting for racial justice and uplifting Black people at every turn.

## Lake Charles

My parents, Alfred and Ruth Mayfield Schexnider, provided a loving home for a big Catholic family of eight at 1708 Winterhalter Street. Before our house was built in 1940, a year after my parents were married, they rented from Mr. and Mrs. William Lancaster, who lived on Magnolia Street, a few blocks from our home. Additions to the house were made as the family grew. The last major addition, a bedroom and a den, occurred in 1950, when my brother Kenneth was born.

Lake Charles was rigidly segregated when I was born, and it wasn't until I was an adult that I realized that Broad Street which ran east and west was the dividing line. Although there were pockets of Whites (Italians and Lebanese) who lived in Black neighborhoods because they owned bakeries, grocery stores, meat markets, and a drug store, most Whites lived south of the acknowledged racial boundary, Broad Street, and Blacks lived north of it.

My childhood was fairly typical of a Black boy growing up in the segregated South in the 1950s and 1960s. My parents poured everything possible into their children. My mother was a homemaker who loved being with her children, cooking, baking, housekeeping, and making sure we had a good life at home and at school. A kind, loving and generous woman who exuded warmth and care, she was totally without guile or pretense and stressed the importance of honesty and integrity. Telling a lie, even a small one was something she could not abide. To this day, I remember her stern warning, "if you lie, you will steal and if you steal you will kill." As a boy, I could not understand the big deal, but as I got older, I began to appreciate that she was trying to instill honesty and integrity. I am not trying to sound saintly, but lying is something I do not do.

I can only use superlatives to describe my mother. She was simply a good person. As an adult, even after I married, I called her every Saturday morning. My father died at the age of 49. For the next twenty-five years, my mother was a widow. After starting a career when I finished college, it was clear that mother needed financial help and I was as supportive as circumstances allowed. I needed her also and I benefited greatly from her love, caring nature, and wisdom. My mother was special, and to this day I miss her very much. My father was a man of few words, so, my mother filled a void. She and I could talk about anything. My father believed that children should be seen and not heard, so he didn't engage us in routine conversation as my mother did. He believed that providing food, shelter, clothing, and school were a show of love. This was difficult for all of us, but I hoped that it would change when we became adults. I believed our communication would have gotten better. By the time I left home at 18, I had learned a lot more from both of my parents than I had ever imagined.

My father was a longshoreman and the breadwinner, so mother did not work outside the home. My father was an excellent provider, and he and my mother made huge sacrifices to ensure the well-being of the family. For example, we attended Sacred Heart School that required tuition and uniforms. My older brothers and I played instruments in the school band, adding more expenses. My sisters and I played on the high school basketball team. My mother would attend games occasionally, but I don't recall my father coming to one. Even though I didn't get to know him as well as I knew my mother,

I idolized my father, admired him greatly and tried to emulate him. There is no doubt that he had a tremendous impact in shaping my character in ways I did not realize until long after he died when I was twenty years old. What I especially remember is that he never raised his voice, he never used profanity and he never repeated himself. Consequently, when Dad spoke we listened.

In spring 1965, I was on Grambling's debate team and during the summer, photographs arrived from our debate against Harvard College. I showed my dad the pictures and he reacted with great pride. My dad was not demonstrative, so witnessing his reaction made me want to work harder. At the end of summer, I returned to college and midway through the semester he died on October 26, 1965.

I was proud of my father. As business agent of the International Longshoremen's (ILA) Local Number 1349 he was one of a handful of Black men in Lake Charles who had an office. He was an influential labor leader who determined which men would work and when, since not all of the stevedores belonged to the union. As a union official, his duties sometimes required business travel to Texas, Alabama, and Florida. It was only after he died that I began to understand that my father was so well respected and revered. At his funeral, for the first time in my life I saw tough, hardcore men cry. Many years later, I was able to understand why: the Port of Lake Charles was the twelfth largest in the country and there was always a need for able-bodied men to load and unload ships. Men seeking work knew they could count on my father to be fair in hiring and to look out for them in negotiating union contracts.

Before he was drafted into the Army in December 1943 my father worked on the docks as a stevedore. During World War II, 700,000 Blacks served in the Army; only 3 percent of these men were in combat units. About 75 percent of Black men served in quarter-master (supply), engineering and transportation units, compared to 40 percent of White men. My father was in the 3236th Quartermaster Service Corps. According to his Army Separation Qualification

Record, my dad was a Duty NCO "in charge of a quartermaster ware-house." During duty in Belgium and France Dad "supervised one hundred fifty soldiers responsible for guarding, loading and unloading Army equipment, rations and supplies from trains and trucks..." One of my prized possessions is the telegram my mother sent to my father, then serving in France, announcing my arrival.

Like my mother, my father was also from a big family. He was born in Lake Charles on February 2, 1916. His parents, Aristele Schexnider and Celestine Joseph Schexnider, were from St. Martin-ville, Louisiana, and moved to Lake Charles in the early 1900s. "Pop," as we called him, died in March 1950. He was the first person I saw in a coffin, and I recall kneeling with my dad as he prayed beside Pop's casket.

My ties to the Catholic Church come from my father's side of the family. My paternal grandmother, Celestine Schexnider, wor-shipped at all–White Immaculate Conception Church in down-town Lake Charles where a special section was reserved for Black Catholics. That was the only option at the time. When Sacred Heart Church opened in 1919, my paternal grandmother was one of the original parishioners. Since then, five generations of the Schexnider family have been baptized and married in the church, and buried in Sacred Heart Cemetery.

My mother was born in Ludington, Louisiana, a hamlet 50 miles northwest of Lake Charles. Her parents, Rufus Mayfield and Arlene Moore Mayfield, had twelve children, including two sets of twins and one set of triplets. My maternal grandfather was from Arkansas as was my maternal grandmother. My grandfather worked for Long Bell Company, a sawmill operation that moved from one state to another as it cleared land. He once told me he could size up a tree and tell how many planks of wood it would produce. I recall him walking with a limp, the result of a sawmill injury. He told me when the acci-dent happened he was taken by horse to the nearest hospital which was in New Orleans. He waited until the doctors got around to treat-ing him, bleeding and in pain for several hours. When he returned to work, he received no compensation for his injuries. Instead, Long Bell offered him employment when the company moved west to Seattle, Washington. My grandmother was intrigued by the idea because she wanted to live in an area where her children could attend college; however, my grandfather passed on the opportunity to move west.

After the youngest of the children, twins Janet and Janice, were born in 1931, he and my grandmother separated, supposedly, over his "fiscal conservatism." My grandfather was proud of the fact that he preferred to save money rather than spend it. According to him, if he allowed it, my grandmother would spend every dime as soon as he brought it home. I just listened and was smart enough never to comment or bring this up to my mother.

My maternal grandmother had a rather privileged life compared to that of my grandfather. Her father, Joel Moore, was a railroad chef enabling him to support his family comfortably. My grandmother attended a boarding school at what is probably Philander Smith College. In the early twentieth century, this was a common practice at newly established Black colleges that offered both "normal" and college preparatory programs. Her plans to go to college were dashed when her father, while working on the railroad as a chef, cut his finger, contracted ptomaine poisoning and died. She was then forced to drop out of school.

A seed had been planted and with unbridled determination Arlene Mayfield with my grandfather's financial support sent her last four children to college. Three graduated and became teachers. One of the four, Arthur Wayne Mayfield, completed a two-year degree at Los Angeles City College, and was admitted to UCLA with plans to complete a bachelor's degree and attend medical school. Instead, when he was discharged from the Army following service in the Korean War he took a job to help support his younger twin sisters who were enrolled at Xavier University in New Orleans, Louisiana. Both graduated and taught in the Lake Charles public schools for over forty years before retiring.

# CHAPTER TWO

# Childhood

One of my earliest recollections is being at home with my mother before starting kindergarten. Our house was about three quarters of a mile south of the Southern Pacific railroad tracks. Hobos, today's homeless, traversed the country by train begging for food along the way. I was with my mother as she ironed clothes in the den, when a scruffy-looking White man appeared at our front door asking for food. My mother, the generous sweet soul that she was, made him a peanut butter and jelly sandwich. That was my first encounter with poverty, and my mother's response left an indelible impression.

My father and his sisters and brothers attended Sacred Heart School; Dad had to drop out in the sixth grade to help support his family.

My father was determined that his children would have opportunities that he was denied so he and my mother enrolled us in Sacred Heart Church and School. This was also the fulfillment of a prior commitment. During that era, because my mother was non–Catholic, my parents could not be married at the altar. Instead, they were married in the Sacristy, where the priests' vestments were kept. This seems harsh and cruel but that was the accepted norm at the time. When my grandmother learned this the day of the wedding, she protested and said had she known this beforehand she would never have consented to the marriage. I have no doubt that she meant it. In addition to being prohibited from saying their vows at the altar, my parents had to pledge that children born of the marriage would be raised Catholic. This is how my school-church journey began.

In 1950, I started kindergarten at Sacred Heart School,

affectionately called "the little red school house" because of its color. Although most of the teachers at Sacred Heart were nuns who belonged to the Sisters of the Blessed Sacrament, some of the teachers were laypersons. In kindergarten, my teacher was Miss Tina Singleton. The classroom seemed big and the playground bigger, but what I remember most about kindergarten was that we had Raisin Bran every day for lunch.

In retrospect, Sacred Heart was good for us. Along with basic subjects (reading, writing, math, and phonics, etc.), we spent considerable time on the Baltimore Catechism. In fact, the Baltimore Catechism was a staple from kindergarten through the 8th grade. When we advanced to Sacred Heart High School, grades 9 through 12, we used a more adult-oriented religious text. In keeping with standard practice, I made my First Holy Communion in the first grade and Confirmation in the seventh.

One of the advantages of attending a small school is that it affords opportunities to be involved in several activities at the same time. In high school I was in the band, the glee club, and played on the basketball team. At six feet, I was a forward and while a mediocre shooter, I was a fairly good rebounder and passer. Since I was in the Glee Club, I was often asked to sing the Dies Irae at funeral Masses, along with my friends, Alex John, Michael Marchand, and Herbert Olivier, with whom I also sang doo-wop songs on the corner after Teen Town on Tuesday and Thursday nights. At that time, Mass and the liturgy were in Latin which helped expand my vocabulary. I also found time to play in a jazz combo composed mainly of airmen at Lake Charles Air Force Base. I was the youngest member of the group, led by Guy Fielder, a Philadelphian who played alto saxophone. I loved jazz, then and now; in hindsight, the airmen tolerated and carried me as I tried to learn the art of improvisation. Playing with these guys was really cool. I learned a lot being in their company and observing their behaviors. Most were from cities on the East Coast, and I admired the way they carried themselves with pride and confidence, despite the segregation they endured in the Air Force and Lake Charles.

Attending Sacred Heart Church and its schools during the 1950s and 1960s in the segregated South was an unforgettable experience. I remember segregated schools, public buildings, restaurants, hotels, and neighborhoods that were off-limits. Although I was a Catholic, I vividly recall the bell tolling at Evergreen Baptist Church, at least a mile or two from our home when a member died. I don't know of any other church with that tradition which I thought was special.

Occasionally, White boys would cruise Black neighborhoods looking for some poor unsuspecting soul to beat up. We were vigilant and always prepared with rocks, bottles, and BB guns. At a very young age, I remember the White paper boy who delivered the *Lake Charles American Press* each day routinely using the N-word until a neighbor shot him with his BB gun. Afterward, we got a Black newspaper delivery boy.

School for me was an unenjoyable experience until the fifth grade. That year, we had five teachers, all laypersons. One gave me an F in math, the only failing grade I ever received. Our last teacher that year was Miss Dolores Tousand. I did well in her class and won a contest for which I received a new baseball mitt. This boosted my confidence considerably. I did not find my sixth grade teacher particularly interested in my academic progress. Things changed noticeably in the seventh grade, where Sister Mary Regina Rosario pressed us hard, but I withstood everything she dished out. Sister Regina had a reputation for being the gatekeeper to entering Sacred Heart High School. Each year, several students failed her class and were either retained for another year or transferred to the public school. Actually, Sister Regina helped build my self-confidence, thereby unlocking my potential as a serious student. Although she was a taskmaster with high standards, Sister Regina had a good sense of humor and smiled with ease. Even in elementary school, I was very serious, but Sister Regina knew how to make me laugh, and started calling me "Happy."

When I was in elementary school, my parents bought my older brother, Alfred Paul, a trombone. I don't think Al was interested in the instrument; thus, Mr. Edward See, our band leader and music teacher, an elderly White man, allowed him to play the bass drum instead. Al let his classmate Timothy Sweet pick up the trombone until my mother found out and dispatched me to retrieve it. Finding students who wanted to learn to play an instrument was not easy, but I jumped at the chance and began lessons. Soon afterward, I was allowed to join the high school band as a sixth-grader and continued until I graduated. Often in the evenings after school, I was exhausted from basketball practice which followed band practice. This meant getting up early the next morning to study. I discovered that my clearest thinking and my best work occurs in the morning. Consequently, to the present, I find mornings the best time to organize my thoughts, reflect, and write.

In 1956, my father bought our first television. It was a Sylvania with a halo light around the 19-inch screen. It was a beautiful piece of furniture and in hindsight it was probably a lemon. Our television seemed to stay in the shop frequently but my dad refused to replace it with another one, probably because he could not afford to. I enjoyed several shows including Pinkie Lee, Howdy Doody, Lassie, Walt Disney and Ed Sullivan shows, Highway Patrol, and westerns. Although the term did not exist at the time, I must have been a nerd because I could not wait to see Lawrence Spivak and *Meet the Press*, every Sunday. I became addicted to politics and public affairs, which likely led to my college and graduate school degrees in political science. I read everything I could find about public affairs, both domestic and foreign.

Acquiring our first television was significant in several respects. In particular, it was television and the era it illuminated that had a huge impact on my growing awareness of the omnipresence of race. I was intellectually curious and enjoyed reading just about anything including magazines and newspapers in addition to school books. Having a television opened new vistas and raised my awareness of escalating racial conflict throughout the South. Lake Charles was segregated but it did not have much of the racial conflict that I saw on television occurring throughout the South, particularly in neighboring Mississippi.

Television may have opened my eyes, so to speak, but the newspaper intrigued me also. I credit my father for the habit of reading the newspaper daily, something I continue to this day. Although he had only a sixth grade education, Dad read two newspapers daily—the *Lake Charles American Press* and the *Beaumont* (Texas) *Enterprise*. On the weekend he added a third, the *New Orleans Times-Picayune*. Watching my father read the newspaper from the front page to the back made a lasting impression on me. As well, reading the newspaper sharpened my awareness of the pervasiveness of race in the country.

By the mid–1950s I was becoming increasingly aware of racial inequalities. In elementary school I recall the 1954 Supreme Court decision, *Brown v. Board of Education of Topeka*. There was no talk of desegregating schools in Lake Charles, but we were fully aware of what it might portend in the distant future. The following year, 1955, a young Baptist preacher launched the Montgomery bus boycott that, although we didn't recognize it at the time, was to have far-reaching implications beyond the capital of Alabama. Blacks across the South were becoming increasingly restive, fed up with seemingly endless acts of White terrorism, sexual abuses, daily insults, taunts, and economic exploitation. As a ten-year-old, I didn't know the full extent of racial discrimination, but Lake Charles, even with its patina of moderation, offered unmistakable clues with segregated schools, churches, public facilities, and everything else. There was even segregation in the delivery of the local newspaper.

One incident in particular is permanently seared into my memory. It occurred in 1955 when I was ten years old. More than any other it fueled my fears and raised my level of awareness about race. At the time, I didn't have a good understanding of race and the justice system but it seemed that something wasn't right about the conviction, and what seemed to me the brutal execution of a Black man. I am referring to the June 1955 execution of Robert Lee Sauls, at the

Calcasieu Parish Jail in Lake Charles, Louisiana. Trying to wrap my mind around the concept of execution was hard, but death by electrocution was even harder for my young, innocent mind to comprehend.[1]

Sauls went to the electric chair insisting that he shot the deputy sheriff in self-defense, but it didn't matter. He was a Black man convicted after two trials of killing a White police officer in the South no less, and again, although it was beyond the comprehension of a ten-year-old, it was unreasonable to expect anything less than a death sentence. Still, that electrocution is permanently etched in memory. Afterward, I became increasingly sensitized to race and the status of Blacks in society. My neighborhood friend, Charles Ray Augustine, went with his family to view the body at Combre Funeral Home, afterward describing a corpse visibly burned. To my knowledge, no one in our family paid a visit.

Reading articles in the *Lake Charles American Press* in which Sauls was described as "the big strapping Negro" or "the husky Corpus Christi Negro," the negative public sentiment against him was palpable. Afterward, the electric chair, which heretofore was portable and moved from one locality to another as needed, was permanently installed at Angola State Prison, which remains to this day one of the world's harshest and most dangerous incarceration facilities in the country.

Lake Charles was no paragon of race relations, but things could have been worse. Stephen Oates notes in his incisive and insightful biography of Martin Luther King, Jr., entitled *Let the Trumpet Sound*, that during the summer of 1955, in one Mississippi city alone, several acts of violence against Blacks were documented:

- May 7, 1955, the Reverend George Lee was murdered because he tried to register Black voters.
- August 13, 1955, Lamar Smith was killed trying to register Black voters.
- December 3, 1955, Clinton Melton was murdered following an argument with a White man at his place of work.

- December 24, 1955, the body of J.E. Evanston, a local school teacher, was discovered in a lake; he was presumably murdered for having the temerity to attend the trial of Emmett Till's murderers.

The United States Supreme Court decision in *Brown v. Board of Education of Topeka*, the Montgomery Bus Boycott and increased agitation for voting rights resulted in even more violence by Whites against Blacks throughout the South. Countless acts of domestic terrorism occurred throughout the country in 1955. One grisly murder, however, had a galvanizing effect on the civil rights movement and that was the lynching of Emmett Till. This is how Oates describes the prelude to a murder:

> a fourteen-year-old Negro who came down from Chicago that summer to visit relatives in Greenwood, Mississippi. One August night three white men dragged him away from a Negro home and flung him into the Tallahatchie River with a seventy-pound cotton gin tied to his neck with barbed wire. The whites murdered him because of a rumor that he had whistled at a white woman. The Brown decision and the white reaction to it, had made national news out of southern racial matters, and numerous outside reporters came to Mississippi for the trial of two of the killers, who of course went free. Why all of this fuss over a dead "nigger" in the Tallahatchie? complained one Mississippi white. That river's full of niggers.[2]

The decision of Emmett Till's mother to have his body displayed in an open coffin caused widespread anger and revulsion. Photographs were displayed in Black newspapers across the country. It created a feeling of anger and disgust that I will never forget. Lake Charles, perhaps because White and Black leaders negotiated behind the scenes, did not, with few exceptions, experience regular racial hostilities probably because there was little agitation for desegregation by Blacks except to integrate McNeese State College. Two blatant acts of racial intimidation I recall included a cross burning by the Ku Klux Klan on the lawn of the local NAACP president who lived on our street and the 1960 disappearance of the only Black man in town who owned a used car business.

Black residents suspected that Richard Antoine, age 41, was abducted by the Klan. When his body was discovered in a bayou on the outskirts of Lake Charles one year later, the coroner concluded, "There are no means of telling if foul play was involved [therefore]... We are going to assume the death was accidental."[3]

There were no additional investigations into Antoine's disappearance and death; however, deep suspicions lingered that he was the victim of foul play for having the temerity to open a business that competed with Whites on the city's main thoroughfare.

During my junior and senior years in high school I was selected to represent Sacred Heart in statewide competition, sponsored by the Louisiana Intercollegiate and Literary Organization (LIALO). This was a novel idea, the brainchild of Black teachers, principals and coaches across Louisiana designed to identify the most talented youth in segregated schools in every city and parish (county). Contestants in various academic subjects met on the campus of Southern University in Baton Rouge. This was my first experience stepping on a Black college campus and I loved it. I represented Sacred Heart High School statewide in the category of Current Events, and placed second in 1962 and first in 1963. Looking back on the LIALO, this was a smart strategy to identify students capable of college study and to encourage them in their academic pursuits. For Southern University, this was an astute enrollment strategy, even though at the time Black colleges and universities had a monopoly on Black students.

For Southern, however, LIALO enabled it to cherry-pick the best and the brightest students and award scholarships. This put Southern University in a very strong competitive position to lure top talent compared to the other Black institutions: Grambling College, Dillard University, and Xavier University. Regrettably, LIALO no longer exists. Its absence, along with the fact that the number of Black teachers and guidance counselors has diminished considerably, means that it is much harder to recruit African American students to Louisiana's Black colleges and universities.

Winning a statewide contest boosted my self-confidence considerably. It also reinforced my ambition and absolute determination to attend college even though I had no idea how I could afford it. I was a strong B+ student, but the school's informal guidance counselor did not encourage me to pursue college. Instead, she encouraged several classmates to enlist in the Air Force and many including some whose grades were better than mine and could easily have done well in college, took her advice and signed up. There was nothing wrong with joining the Air Force or any branch of the service for that matter; it was simply not something I wanted to do at the time.

If a Sacred Heart student did go to college the nuns felt obligated to steer them to Xavier University in New Orleans whose founder, St. Katharine Drexel, also established the Sisters of the Blessed Sacrament. The nuns who taught at Sacred Heart and several other Black Catholic schools in the South belonged to that Order. Attending a secular or non–Catholic college was strongly discouraged by the nuns who taught us which, of course, only heightened my interest in attending one. I subsequently applied to one college, Tennessee State A & I University in Nashville, where a cousin, Anthony Thomas, had graduated. I was admitted but neither financial aid nor campus housing was available, so I did not go. At the time nothing was more important to me than going to college but I simply didn't have the money.

My graduation from Sacred Heart coincided with my eighteenth birthday. I celebrated it by taking my first flight on an airplane. My friend and fellow classmate from kindergarten through the twelfth grade, Carl Ross, joined me in flying from Lake Charles to Houston on Trans-Texas Airways, dubbed Tree Top Airways by the locals. My dad's oldest brother, Uncle Joe, treated us to a Houston Astros baseball game. I don't know about Carl but I didn't have enough money to return by plane so we took the Greyhound bus back home. Still, it was an exciting and memorable day. In September, Carl enrolled at

Southern University and a handful of classmates entered other colleges. I felt left out but I was determined that I would eventually go to college, graduate and start a career.

For a host of reasons 1960s was an interesting era, not only because of the civil rights movement, but also because of what was occurring in the national and international arena. The John F. Kennedy administration ushered in a New Frontier and with it confrontations with the Soviet Union. The Bay of Pigs invasion in 1961, occurring just one year after Kennedy took office, was a huge blunder and perhaps the worst mistake of his administration. Under Kennedy's authorization and coordinated by the Central Intelligence Agency, a group of Cuban exiles attempted to overthrow Fidel Castro but failed. This fiasco led to increasing tension not only with Cuba but also with the Soviet Union since Cuba was among its client states. The conflict escalated and with it the potential for war with a small country ninety miles off the American shore. Fidel Castro, no ordinary dictator, was as powerful a foe as the United States would have.

The discovery of Soviet-deployed missiles in Cuba resulted in a Navy blockade. Tense negotiations in the United Nations resulted in an exceptional speech by Adlai Stevenson, Jr., United States Ambassador to the United Nations and former Governor of Illinois, in which he demanded to know whether weapons existed on the island. It was a type of political theater I had never witnessed. Each day I rushed home to watch the evening news and to read the *Lake Charles American Press*. This was a real test of who held the balance of power in the world and President Kennedy knew that he dare not blink first.

In addition to the fact that the Soviets backed down from the threat of a potential nuclear war, what I remember most about the incident is Valerian Aleksandrovich Zorin, the Russian ambassador, obfuscating and dancing around rather than answering the question about the existence of the missiles and Ambassador Stevenson saying, "I am prepared to wait for my answer until hell freezes over." Stevenson had evidence of the missiles in Cuba, but what he wanted was a public acknowledgment and shaming of our main nemesis. For a high school student whose appetite for public affairs was insatiable, I loved every moment of the drama.

Another great desire of mine in 1963 after graduating Sacred Heart was to participate in the March on Washington. College students were participating in sit-ins and protests across the country and I very much wanted to be a part of the movement. The March on Washington had been heralded as a pivotal moment, a turning point, and a once in a lifetime opportunity to join with people from across the country in support of civil rights and equality of opportunity. As much as I wanted to I couldn't attend this one either. There were probably others in Lake Charles who participated in the March on Washington in 1963, but the only person I knew who attended was my friend and classmate, Carl Ross. I admit to being somewhat envious, but I was pleased that my friend was a part of that historic gathering.

Since I couldn't afford to go to college after graduating from Sacred Heart, in September 1963, I decided to move to New York, where I stayed with an aunt and uncle in Queens. Shortly after I arrived I found a job as a clerk at Hockaday and Associates, an advertising agency in Manhattan on the corner of Madison Avenue and 57th Street. I rode the subway each day to the city and quickly began to learn my way around it. I was fascinated by the Big Apple—its people, sounds, smells but especially its vibrancy. I loved live entertainment and found my way to Birdland and the Village Gate and attended jazz sessions as often as my limited finances would allow. While roaming Manhattan on separate occasions I also met Jackie Robinson and Sidney Poitier. I could hardly contain my excitement at meeting them; both were affable and greeted me kindly.

The 1963–1964 year in New York was filled with adventure, but also tragedy. On November 22, 1963, President John F. Kennedy was assassinated. The office closed early and along with hundreds of others, I went to St. Patrick's Cathedral to pray. The assassination occurred on a Friday and the entire weekend the nation was fixated on televised events in Dallas and Washington. The office was closed

Monday, so along with the nation, I watched more television and witnessed Lee Harvey Oswald being transported by Dallas police, when, he too, was killed by Jack Ruby.

In January 1964, I enrolled in two courses at Queens College in Flushing, New York. I enjoyed being back in school among students with similar aspirations. I especially enjoyed my English composition course, taught by Mr. Bernard Katz, who commented on an essay that my writing was "good, but erratic." I wish I had asked him to explain.

It did not take long to realize that pursuing a college degree part-time was not going to work for me. My grandmother, Arlene Mayfield, visited New York in spring of 1964 and urged me to find a way to enroll in college as a full-time student. Someone had told her about Long Island University and while this may have been a good idea I did not have the resources to go anywhere as a full-time student. I was also homesick and began thinking about returning to Louisiana. My brother Al told me this would mean regressing and advised against it. Still, I did not like the idea of working and going to college part-time. It required considerable energy and it would take too long to finish. Mainly, though, I felt I was missing out on life as a college student on a campus. This was during the height of the civil rights movement and Black college students were on the vanguard. I wanted to be a part of something much bigger than Queens College could offer.

I do not recall the circumstances but somehow Grambling College entered the picture. An uncle through marriage, L. Joseph Sanford, had graduated from Grambling. I also knew several Grambling alums who were teachers and coaches in Lake Charles. I wrote for a catalog and an application. At the time, tuition, room and board cost $300. I had saved a little more than half of that amount and with help from my parents, and Uncle Rufus and Aunt Marion Mayfield and Aunt Fritz and Uncle Bob Forbes, who gave $50 each, I met my target. Thus, I entered Grambling College in September 1964, with just enough money, $300, to cover one semester—along with pocket change. I was convinced that if I got my foot in the door, I would be fine.

My pent-up desire to be in college and a lot of prayers paid off. I discovered a small Catholic chapel on Park Avenue, not far from where I worked, and I attended Mass there almost daily, praying that I would be able to enroll in college in the fall. Without a doubt my faith, "the substance of things hoped for, the evidence of things unseen," sustained me and I will never forget it.

I had a lot of ambition when I started college and completed my first semester on the dean's list. Being a good student and participating in one or two campus activities garnered a lot of attention from faculty and students. In order to continue the next semester, I applied for and received a National Defense Student Loan in the amount of $300. Again I made the dean's list, which Grambling recognized by awarding me a merit scholarship for the second year. I could not have been happier. In spring 1965, I joined the debate team and was elected vice president of the Student Government Association (SGA), only the second freshman to have won that position in the history of the college, putting me on the path to becoming SGA President my junior year. I was also active in the Newman Club, an organization of Catholics on campus, and later was elected its president. Clearly, my prayers, hard work and self-confidence were paying off in ways I could not have imagined.

## Summer of 1965

Summer 1965 was memorable in good ways, but it was also heartbreaking and sad. In retrospect, I am confident it was divine Providence that returned me to Louisiana, after one year in New York. When the spring semester ended, I knew that I had funding for the 1964–65 school year. Black Greek organizations came calling and I decided to pledge Alpha Phi Alpha Fraternity. The pledge period began in late spring and was to continue, pending good grades, into the fall semester.

**Officers of the Grambling College Newman Club. Left to right: Lillian Dodd, Father Kevin Roe, Alvin Schexnider, Marilyn Edwards, Maxime Robertson, Grambling College, 1968 (author's collection).**

At age 13, I started working at my Uncle Rufus Mayfield's business, Esquire Cleaners. After school and during summers, I had a job that ensured I had pocket change to buy clothes, and go to movies and Teen Town. I learned to save and opened an account at Gulf National Bank. I also developed a good work ethic. With one exception, each summer I returned to Lake Charles and worked at my uncle's dry cleaners.

In February 1965, Uncle Rufus and Aunt Marion bought a new 1965 Oldsmobile 98 Luxury Sedan in order to drive to Los Angeles for a summer vacation. My uncle asked if I felt comfortable managing the business while they were away, and I assured him I could handle it. They left and arrived in Los Angeles just as the Watts Riot started. This was not the greeting they expected, but they enjoyed the trip in their beautiful and comfortable land yacht, nonetheless.

In addition, in the summer of 1965, my mother and younger sister and brother, Sandra and Kenneth traveled to New York to attend my sister Manella's wedding, and to attend the New York World's Fair, which was in its second and final year. That meant that my father and I were home alone that summer. Maybe because I was a young adult or perhaps it was because he saw me as a mature college student, but whatever the reason, I was able to communicate with him better than I had before. My dad was taciturn, rarely showing emotion and more inclined to give directions than show his emotions. It was much later in life that I realized that he was basically shy, as am I.

With a large family, my dad was never able to buy a new car. He and my mother sacrificed to send us to Catholic school. He was the sole breadwinner, so I am sure this was a factor. I am eternally grateful to them. The closest my father came to owning a new car was when he bought a 1964 Pontiac Bonneville. It was a "demo" that dealers used for test drives for prospective buyers. It was a beautiful car and had never been titled. Unfortunately, he was not able to enjoy it for long.

That summer, while my mother and younger siblings were away, my father developed a cough that would not go away. He tried several home remedies before going to his doctor who initially diagnosed walking pneumonia. Prescription drugs did not help, so in late August, I drove him to St. Patrick's Hospital where he had a biopsy. Frankly, I was young, naïve and clueless about my father's health. When my Uncle Rufus and Aunt Marion returned in August, my father came to the cleaners one day to pick up his laundry. My dad's daily uniform was khaki pants starched with a sharp crease. He was a tall, handsome guy who cut an impressive figure no matter what he wore and even in khakis he was cool.

When my father walked into the cleaners, Uncle Rufus knew immediately that he was seriously ill. I had previously gotten a clue at Aunt Rosa's when he had trouble starting his lawn mower, but I did not recognize it. Aunt Rosa was deeply bothered seeing him struggle to start the lawn mower and asked me to relieve him because it was obvious that he lacked the strength to pull the rope cord. I got the lawn mower started, even as it hurt my father's pride. Still, I did not know that he was gravely ill.

My uncle asked my Aunt Janice to call my mother to tell her she should come home because my father was sick. Not long afterwards, my mother, Kenneth, and Sandra took the train home. He paid my uncle, Johnnie Teat, to drive to New Orleans to pick them up because he lacked the energy to do it himself. For a man of his pride and independence to ask someone to drive to New Orleans to pick up his wife and children should have alerted me about his health but it had not.

After my mother's return from New York, my dad's health continued to decline. As planned, I returned to Grambling in September. My father was home when friends picked me up in a compact Oldsmobile F-85 for the trip back to Grambling. He expressed concern about my safety in a small car packed to the hilt. I assured him that we would be fine, and I greatly appreciated this rare display of emotion.

One night in September, my mother woke up to find my dad sitting at the dining room table with his head resting on his arms. Fluid had begun to fill his lungs and this was the only way he could try to sleep. My mother was alarmed and pressed him to tell her what was going on with his health. Finally, he admitted that he had been diagnosed with lung cancer. When she asked why he had not told her, he said he simply could not bring himself to have that conversation. He began radiation treatment shortly afterward.

In late October, my Uncle Rufus called and told me I should come home. He did not elaborate why, but I knew it had to be serious. My father died on October 26, 1965. My older brothers, Thad and Al, were with him when he passed at St. Patrick's Hospital. When they called to tell my mother we should come quickly, I sensed that this did not bode well. We entered the hospital room and there he lay, lifeless, his body still warm. I kissed him, said a prayer, removed his wedding band, and gave it to my mother. For the first fourteen years of my marriage, I did not wear a wedding band. When my mother died in 1992, I retrieved my dad's ring and I have worn it since, with enormous pride.

I credit my grandmother, Arlene Mayfield, with encouraging me to excel in school and to attend college. Her four youngest children went to college, and three graduated and became teachers largely because of her determination. When one considers all the barriers to success Black people experienced prior to the civil rights era, one can appreciate the significance of this remarkable accomplishment. Scholarships were rare, and grants and student loans were nonexistent. While it helped to be smart and determined, hard work and family support were critical. Sometimes the local church helped, but mainly students and their families were on their own in the pursuit of a college degree. My grandparents worked hard and made huge sacrifices so that their daughters would not have to work in some White family's home as domestics.

Early on, my grandmother, "Miss Arlene," saw potential in me. When I was eleven years old, she entered me into an oratorical contest sponsored by the American Woodmen's Association, a fraternal insurance company. My uncle L. Joseph Sanford helped me write a speech. This was my first foray into public speaking, a skill I honed in college as a member of Grambling's debate team. I gave my speech at the local Masonic temple and placed second. My grandmother was convinced I would have won but for the prejudice of the judges whom she was convinced were enamored with the attractiveness of a female contestant who was declared the winner. I was happy to have finished as runner-up because it boosted my pride and self-confidence.

Years later after completing graduate school and starting my academic career my grandmother continued to show interest in me. She was a very wise woman whom I always enjoyed listening to and from whom I learned a lot about life. Late one afternoon in June 1980, she called to tell me that she had just returned from a wedding with my Aunt Janet, one of the twins. She remarked that Janet had on the same dress she had worn to my wedding to Virginia two years earlier. Her main reason for calling was to tell me the following:

- She wanted Virginia and me to know she was thinking about us, that she loved us and was very proud of us.
- She loved all her children and did not intend to prepare a will. Her house would be left to whomever wished to use it.
- Her greatest joy came from her children and grandchildren, and
- No matter what happened, she loved us.

I recorded notes from this phone call on June 28, 1980, at 5:30 p.m. For more than 40 years, they have been securely filed as I moved several times in pursuit of a career. Memories of that phone call and these notes remain among my most prized possessions.

As I reflect on this experience six decades later, I view it as the beginning of my ability to excel if I worked hard and applied myself. This was validated in high school where I had classmates whom I believed were smarter in subjects like algebra, trigonometry and chemistry, but no one worked harder than I did. I earned good grades because I had grit and determination. Even though I was often too tired to study after basketball practice, I would get up early the next morning and hit the books. Nearly all of my classmates were really smart and could easily have done well in college. Several joined the military instead.

At Sacred Heart, I also encountered the phenomenon of "colorism," or intra-group discrimination based on skin tone, and how it shaped views about intelligence and academic achievement. In the 1960s, Sacred Heart was relatively small compared to the two Black public high schools, W.O. Boston and Washington. Between 1959 and 1963, Sacred Heart High School's total enrollment, I doubt, exceeded 200 students. My senior class, for example, had a total of 24 students, almost evenly divided between boys and girls.

Sacred Heart School, like much of south Louisiana, had an

abundance of Creoles many of whom, but not all, were light-complexioned. Some could and attempted to pass for White, a practice referred to as passé blanc. I know of several from Sacred Heart who moved to California, crossed over and never returned to Lake Charles. Not all Creoles were of this mindset, but many seized the opportunity to step into a different reality. Sometimes the nuns and priests showed partiality to lighter-complexioned schoolmates, even to the point of presuming they were innately smarter. This manifested itself in fostering vocations to the priesthood or a religious order, as well as in academic recognition, unless a darker complexioned student was unequivocally superior.

My older brother, Alfred, dark complexioned like me, was especially sensitive to this pernicious behavior, so in the sixth grade he organized his buddies to elect a dark-complexioned girl class queen to the consternation of several students and the teacher, Sister Mary Raphael, who promptly reported him to my father. My dad listened politely but did not remonstrate with Al or discipline him because he knew my brother and his friends had a little fun at the expense of students who were prejudiced against their darker-skinned classmates.

# Chapter Three

# Grambling College
# 1964–1968

In September 1964, I left Penn Station, New York, headed to Grambling, Louisiana, to enroll at Grambling College. I had never been to north Louisiana, let alone set foot on Grambling's campus. Although Louisiana was thoroughly segregated, the southern part of the state was less harsh and hostile toward its Black citizens. Attending college was my number one priority and I was determined to succeed. Both at home and at school, I had been told, "where there is a will there is a way," and "God helps those who help themselves." I took all of this in, so there was never any doubt that once I got to college, I was going to excel and I did.

Following my first year at Grambling and in the summer of 1965 I also enrolled in one course at McNeese State College to get a head start on the next year. I had not decided on a major although my Uncle Rufus was urging me to study business, which frankly, I found uninteresting. Increasingly, I was inclined toward the liberal arts, a new area of concentration at Grambling and one that I found more intellectually challenging. I felt confident and self-assured.

During my freshman year I joined the Grambling debate team and participated in the Grambling–Harvard debate on a sunny spring Sunday afternoon. The debate team helped to expand my horizon and it bolstered my confidence. It also honed my critical thinking skills, and it improved my written and verbal communication.

Although no winner was declared, at the end our debate coach, Mr. George Wesley, was pleased that we had acquitted ourselves well. Following the debate, we had a reception and took pictures with the Harvard debate team. I learned later that this was one of several Harvard debate teams and that this one, perhaps inspired by the civil rights movement, chose to schedule debates on a tour of colleges and universities in the South.

My four years at Grambling College will always be special, perhaps because I had to work so hard to get there. I always knew that I wanted to go to college, but after graduating from Sacred Heart, I lacked the means to enroll anywhere with the exception of McNeese State College in Lake Charles. In 1963, Black students could attend McNeese, but they were prohibited from living on campus and participating in extra-curricular activities. It was simply go to class, take courses and leave. That was not the kind of college experience I wanted and frankly, it was not the type of situation that I felt was conducive to my personal and professional growth and development. I yearned to play on a bigger field with students who came from across the country and with whom I believed I had more in common.

Although Grambling is situated in fairly remote rural and highly conservative north Louisiana, thanks to the news media, we were fully aware of the movement and the war. Some classmates were drafted or enlisted. Student activism in civil rights at Grambling was sparse, although occasionally we would hear about individual acts of courage by a student here or there. Overall, I recall very little in the way of organized protest. One incident I heard about that has haunted me all these years is about a Grambling student who died trying to desegregate a local restaurant in his hometown.

I did not know him personally, but according to rumor, he lived in a small town not far from Grambling. One day he went to a local White café and ordered a cup of coffee. He was refused service and left. He returned the next day and this time received service. Shortly afterward, he became violently ill and died from what was believed to have been by poisoning. I do not recall anyone ever being arrested, charged or prosecuted. This would not have been unusual at that time and in the northern region of Louisiana, especially, where the Ku Klux Klan was known to be active. In many rural areas of the state Whites dominated every aspect of political and economic life and the most basic civil and human rights of Black people were routinely ignored. If your mother worked as a domestic and your father worked at the local sawmill, equal protection under the law was nonexistent. The Ku Klux Klan and local law enforcement might be and were often the same.

Grambling is a public institution and its president in keeping with the tenor and times of segregation was not one to buck the system. Some Black college presidents at the time stood behind students who protested for civil rights. However, if a Grambling student challenged the system, he or she was pretty much on their own. Student activism was discouraged. Of course, Black students at many colleges across the South protested aggressively. The Student Nonviolent Coordinating Committee (SNCC) emerged from the civil rights movement and many Black and White students were involved in the Southern Christian Leadership Conference (SCLC). At Grambling, however, we were mostly silent.

For the 1965–66 school year I was vice president of the Student Government Association (SGA) while a third-year student from Jonesboro, Louisiana, was president. That spring, without consulting its officers, the SGA president decided to organize a demonstration to extend the hours of the library to give students more time to study. I wasn't excited about leading a demonstration since I had just buried my dad and I was trying to catch up on my studies. Nonetheless, given my position, I felt compelled to support what I considered a worthy cause. Extending library hours was like motherhood and apple pie. Who would oppose that? On the face of it, and certainly at a time when students across the country were protesting with more strident demands, this did not seem to be asking too much. This was hardly a threat to the established order, but at Grambling where protest of any type was forbidden, the administration took great umbrage at the very idea of organized protest.

The SGA was unable to draw significant support of the protest. After a few days, the president of the college summoned the SGA leaders to his office and informed us that we would be expelled if we did not end the demonstration. For me, this was a no-brainer since we never got any traction and I wanted to focus on my studies. Knowing how hard I had worked to get to Grambling the threat did not take much convincing. I walked away and the others did too, albeit reluctantly. The SGA president was deeply involved in demonstration activities, so much in fact, that at the end of the semester he flunked out. My grades had suffered but I was nowhere close to academic probation or suspension. In fact, my grades were strong enough to retain my merit scholarship. I decided to decline the scholarship the following year in favor of a job as a resident assistant in one of the dormitories. This position covered tuition, room and board, and I kept it for the remaining two years at Grambling.

During the fall 1967, my senior year, students became disenchanted with the excessive emphasis on athletics over academics. A student protest led by the president of the Student Government Association drew wide campus support. It was the first time a broad scale student-organized protest occurred at Grambling and it was for good cause. That the issue of athletics superseding academic pursuits was inspired and led by students rather than faculty, staff or alumni spoke volumes. This should have been an embarrassment and a wakeup call to the college's administration, but the student protests fell on deaf ears. I believed then and now that excessive attention to athletics over academic considerations tends to hinder a university's development as an institution of higher learning.

Even with some of the longest running and largest HBCU intercollegiate sporting events in the world, many schools have been unable to translate these activities into major financial gains. The Bayou Classic, for example, has been running for more than fifty years and in the past has drawn more than 100,000 attendees to New Orleans, a city well-known for tourism, hospitality and entertainment. Even though the Bayou Classic is more than half a century old, the extent of financial gain derived from it by its two competitors, Grambling State University and Southern University, is unclear.

Ideally, athletic events like the Bayou Classic could serve to enhance academic programs and to create scholarships for deserving students. Revenues from annual classics could be used for a variety of goals including funding scholarships and boosting retention and graduation rates. These factors are especially important since increasingly states apply metrics like retention and graduation rates to shape budget decisions. In other words, a public college or university that has an acceptable graduation rate is viewed more favorably than one that does not. Legislators often view strong retention and graduation rates as a positive return on investment. Historically Black Colleges and Universities (HBCUs) may claim special treatment because of their mission, historic inequities in funding and the type of student they enroll; however, that argument is an increasingly difficult one since 90 percent of Black students attend White colleges and universities and their graduation rates are often similar to those of the majority of students.

## Chapter Four

# Launching a Career

My college years paralleled the civil rights movement and the Vietnam War. It was a fascinating time for a young Black man graduating from college, trying to start a career and leaving the family nest all under the looming cloud of conscription. While at Grambling, I had received four deferments from my local draft board. I was convinced that I was going to be drafted and sent to Vietnam.

In the mid–1960s, Black urban discontent resulted in riots in several major American cities—Los Angeles, Cleveland, Newark, and Detroit. Civil rights leaders aggressively pushed to expand job opportunities in the public and private sectors for Blacks across the country. Consequently, major corporations began recruiting on Black college campuses. President Lyndon Johnson, for example, prevailed upon Henry Ford II, president of Ford Motor Company, to lead the National Alliance for Business (NAB). Its mission was to increase job opportunities for Blacks in the private sector. Ford Motor Company recruited several Grambling schoolmates to work in Detroit. One of my fraternity brothers, Floyd Washington, after graduating from Grambling, went on to earn an MBA from the University of Chicago. Floyd was one of the first Black college alums hired as an executive at Ford Motor Company.

In the summer of 1967, I worked as an intern at the headquarters of the Social Security Administration in Baltimore, Maryland. The recruiter, Frank Eife, after interviewing several rising seniors at Grambling, selected me for the internship with the prospect of hiring upon graduation the following year. Mr. Eife was also instrumental in finding a family for me to stay with during the three months of the internship. I was assigned to work in human resources with

Alma Baer, who was very kind and helpful. I helped her with filing and tracking claims and handling basic administrative tasks. Mainly, the internship provided a glimpse into the inner workings of a huge governmental bureaucracy.

At the end of the summer, Alma asked me what I thought about working for the Social Security Administration. Never one to mask feelings, my lack of enthusiasm was evident and before I could answer, Alma said she doubted I would be happy working there. She was right. When the recruiter from Owens-Illinois came to campus during my senior year and interviewed me for a personnel trainee position, almost immediately I began thinking about what it would be like to work in a major corporation doing something entirely different from the jobs most Blacks were confined to at the time.

My mother's youngest sisters were schoolteachers and so were their husbands. They strongly urged me to avoid teaching and seek job opportunities in the private sector. Actually, I was never interested in teaching anyway, so it did not take much convincing. In high school, I believed I wanted to follow in the footsteps of my dad who was the business agent for his union local. This goal, noted in my senior yearbook, was to become a labor mediator. This was as close to my father's vocation as I could get. I wrote to Cornell University and New York University seeking catalogs that described their degree programs in labor and industrial relations where both were reputed leaders. I could not afford to enroll in either school, but that did not stop me from dreaming and inquiring. Consequently, when I chose a major at Grambling, I knew that I wanted to work in business and industry; teaching was never on my horizon and during four years of college, I did not take one course in teacher education. Instead, I was among the first to enroll in Grambling's new bachelor of arts degree program with a concentration in political science.

I graduated from Grambling College on May 26, 1968, my twenty-third birthday. (Incidentally, I graduated from Sacred Heart High School on May 26, 1963, my eighteenth birthday.) I started my new job as a personnel trainee at Owens-Illinois one week later. The corporate headquarters of Owens-Illinois was located in Toledo, Ohio. Owens-Illinois manufactured boxes for its sister glass company, Owens-Corning. The executive who recruited me, Robert Frane, was my supervisor, mentor, and guide throughout my three-month training program.

Toledo was a medium-size city with a corporate presence and a working-class feel to it. Because of its proximity to Detroit, Toledo was a manufacturing center for automotive parts. It was home to the Willys car company, manufacturer of the Jeep and a key player in the wartime production of vehicles. Thankfully, I did not stay in Toledo long for it did not seem to have much to offer socially.

After completing my training program, I was transferred to a box manufacturing plant on the outskirts of Detroit. Owens-Illinois had plants all over the country so, after my training program was completed, I could have been transferred to any of them. Two that were mentioned as possibilities were the island of Abaco in the Bahamas and another in Valdosta, Georgia. Neither excited me, but the prospect of being transferred to Valdosta, Georgia, did give me pause.

I arrived in Detroit, Michigan, around Labor Day and found an apartment downtown not far from the headquarters of General Motors. This was an interesting time to be in Detroit. A huge race riot had occurred in the summer of 1967, resulting in 43 casualties and substantial damage due to burnings and destruction of property downtown. Detroit, like the average American city, had its share of racial problems. Racial discrimination was still palpable. Blacks felt the heat of oppression and police brutality was routine. When I arrived, the city was still tense one year later. I recall walking downtown and seeing White women clutching their purse as they approached me on the sidewalk.

Detroit won the World Series that year and winning the pennant allowed the city to release a lot of pent-up tension and energy. Now, there was something everyone in the entire city could celebrate. Police cars and fire trucks with sirens screaming raced through the city's streets with abandon. It was quite a sight to behold, but a welcome catharsis for everyone in the aftermath of the 1967 riot.

I did not have a car so I rode the bus to and from work each day. After work I often stopped by the General Motors showroom on the first floor where all the new car models were on display. I never tired of closely inspecting the new Chevrolet, Pontiac, Oldsmobile, Buick and Cadillac cars. For as long as I could remember, I was enamored with cars yet I was intent on saving until I could afford to buy and maintain one. In college, Lathardus Goggins, a geography professor, owned three cars: a new Jaguar XKE, a Porsche 356 and a 1954 Austin Healy 3000. He drove a different one each day and I could hardly contain my excitement when I saw one of them.

One day he offered to sell me the Austin Healy for $350. This was a great bargain, but I did not have the money. I probably could have borrowed it from my Aunt Marion and Uncle Rufus, but even if they had agreed, I knew that I could not afford to maintain a fancy sports car. As much as I love cars I am not mechanically inclined, and then as now, I lacked the skills to do even basic repairs and tune-ups. Now that I was out of college and earning a decent salary, this seemed to be a good time to think about buying a new car as many of my friends had done. It was probably a good idea that I rode the bus to work and did not buy a car as badly as I wanted one. My days at Owens-Illinois and in Detroit were to be short-lived. Six months after graduating Grambling, I received a notice of induction into the United States Army. I was to report to Fort Bliss, Texas, on December 13, 1968.

My military tour of duty began less than two weeks before Christmas. This was during a period of heightened emphasis on the draft, given the mounting casualties in Vietnam. The Tet Lunar offensive in 1968 raised serious doubts about our military's ability to successfully prosecute the Vietnam War. Anti-war protests occurred simultaneously with civil rights demonstrations across the country. Race riots in several major American cities—Newark, New Jersey; Washington, D.C.; Cleveland, Ohio; and Detroit, Michigan, along with a major protest against the war during the Democratic National

Convention in 1968—provided a backdrop to racial unrest not just in the country but within the armed forces as well.

My basic training was at Fort Bliss, Texas. One of my most poignant but disturbing experiences was to discover that my basic training officer proudly displayed a Confederate license plate on his car. One day I challenged him about it and asked him how he thought I felt having been drafted into the Army while he was still fighting the Civil War? He said he did not care if I supported Martin Luther King so I should not care if he had a Confederate license plate on his car. I told him there was no comparison. We butted heads the entire time I was in basic training.

Afterward, I was sent to Fort Huachuca, Arizona, for advanced individual training in the Army Signal Corps. We were taught Morse code before being sent to units at various commands. After completing the course, many soldiers were assigned as radiomen in Vietnam. At the time I was drafted, I believed I would ultimately end up in Vietnam, which I did although later than I expected. After my training at Fort Huachuca, I was assigned there as an instructor. Some of my fellow soldiers also spent their tours of duty there as instructors. I have no idea why some stayed and others were posted elsewhere. After a year, I was sent to Vietnam, even though I only had nine months of service left before being discharged.

Before deployment to Vietnam, I was allowed to see my family in Lake Charles. Following a brief visit I left for the Oakland Army Base in California. While waiting to leave I visited my Aunt Leana Schexnider Welch, my father's older sister who lived in San Francisco. I had met her many years before and was happy to see her since she was unable to attend my father's funeral in October 1965. She told me how much she admired my dad and the great time they had when he visited in 1962. She gave me a picture of her and my father and the children taken during his visit. She and the children, Gloria, Sharon and Jesse, took me to lunch at Arthur Treacher's seafood restaurant. I had heard about Arthur Treacher's fish and chips. I enjoyed the meal well enough, but it was not like the fresh seafood I took for granted back home.

In the 1960s, the shipping industry was changing, specifically moving from manual labor toward mechanization to load and unload ships. As a union official my father was assigned by the International Longshoreman's Association (ILA) to serve on a nationwide task force to conduct a feasibility study. My great-uncle, Wilmer H. Hopkins (my maternal grandmother's brother), held a very high position as Assistant Secretary-Treasurer of the ILA's Gulf Coast District. Uncle Wilmer was based in Houston and was a vice president of the AFL-CIO. I am pretty sure Uncle Wilmer was responsible for my father's appointment to the task force in 1962 that visited major ports in the United States examining the emerging role of containerized cargo in the shipping industry.

Appointment to the task force enabled my dad to review operations at the Port of San Francisco; while there he was able to visit his sister, Aunt Leana and her family. Then the task force examined operations at the Port Authority of New York and New Jersey. This trip enabled him to visit my brother and sisters in New York. Albeit brief, his trip to New York provided an opportunity for him to spend time with my sisters Lois, Louise, and Manella, who had moved to New York only a few months earlier. My sisters were able to see him in a different light; he danced with each of them and showed a side of himself he had kept hidden.

## Vietnam

I arrived in Phu Bai, Vietnam, in March 1970, during the monsoon season. It rained daily and it was cold and dark. I was assigned as a radioman to a combat construction-engineering unit thirty miles from the Demilitarized Zone (DMZ). Because I was in the company headquarters, I had no field duties. Combat units of the 101st Airborne, known as the Screaming Eagles, and some Marines were also posted in Phu Bai, which was 12 miles from Hue where the Tet Lunar Offensive occurred.

My personal goal in Vietnam was to stay safe and alive. On the day I arrived a Black soldier was being sent home because he had a nervous breakdown. I remember that his name was "Hilton" and he was from Memphis, Tennessee. He was tall and lanky with a faraway look in his eyes. After a few nights there, I began to understand how he may have had a nervous breakdown.

Phu Bai regularly received incoming mortar rounds from the Viet Cong. We never knew when to expect them and where they would land. It was unsettling and fearful and caused a lot of tension. Everyone wanted to stay alive and particularly as the time neared for a soldier to leave Vietnam fears and anxieties increased. I understood "Hilton's" anxieties and said to myself, "there but for the grace of God go I."

My time in Vietnam brought no relief from racial tensions. The riots that occurred during the 1960s in Cleveland, Detroit, Gary and Newark were partly spawned by the Black Power movement. It also raised public awareness about the disproportionate number of Black casualties during the War. As a soldier, I witnessed and experienced a lot. Black authors were writing both fiction and facts about the Black experience in a variety of settings and contexts. One in particular that grabbed my attention was a book by two psychiatrists practicing in San Francisco, William H. Grier and Price Cobbs. Their book and these words resonated with me and crystallized my thoughts succinctly: "For white America to understand the Black man, it must recognize that so much time has passed and so little has changed."[1] Yes, the civil rights movement had brought change, but here I was fighting a war I didn't believe in, Black soldiers were still being mistreated, and like my father, a veteran of World War II, I would return, if lucky, to face more racism after being discharge.

The armed services were desegregated by Executive Order 9981 issued by President Harry Truman in 1948. The Korean War helped to facilitate its implementation. Integration in the military occurred faster than in civilian society but it was slow nonetheless. Consequently, by the time of the Vietnam War, almost twenty years after Truman's order, the persistence of racial inequities throughout the armed services was laid bare. As Muhammad Ali reminded America, combating racism while fighting in a war against people who had never mistreated him made no sense. Ali paid a huge price for refusing the draft but the symbolism for Black soldiers and civilians was powerful.

Experiencing racism in Vietnam and reading about racial problems at home gave rise to racial solidarity among Black soldiers in Vietnam and in Europe. In Vietnam it was common to see Black servicemen (soldiers, sailors, airmen and marines) exchanging "dap," intricate handshakes and greetings, wearing amulets on their wrists and wearing huge Afro hairstyles often in violation of military guidelines. Each branch of the services issued guidelines about hair length but Black soldiers largely ignored them. Racial pride and racial solidarity with the civil rights movement at home was openly expressed even though it made Whites uncomfortable. Also fueling the fire were resentments that Black soldiers were disproportionately represented in war casualties and fatalities. Racism at home and racism while defending the country was too much to bear.

I experienced racism in Vietnam but I don't recall any physical altercations between Black and White soldiers in my Signal Corps unit. There is no doubt that the Vietnam War caused racial solidarity and Black pride in the military. For me personally, it strengthened my resolve to do everything possible to uplift Blacks when I returned to civilian society.

Perhaps the greatest toll the Vietnam War had on Black soldiers—and all soldiers for that matter—were the aftereffects, namely post-traumatic stress syndrome, or PTSD as it is commonly called. That is likely what I saw in the Black soldier who was leaving my unit the day I arrived in Vietnam. I had witnessed a similar incident but didn't understand it. As we were leaving the Oakland Army Base in California, I witnessed a Black soldier having a nervous breakdown. He had just left where we were going, Vietnam. Sadly, many of today's homeless are Vietnam War veterans who bear scars and wounds that seem never to heal.

While my unit did not see combat, we were subjected to intermittent mortar rounds during the day and at night. We never knew when or where a mortar might hit which made for an unsettling experience. This continued throughout my time in Vietnam. Thankfully, I did not have to complete the nine months left on my enlistment. That is because at the time the armed services allowed enlisted personnel and commissioned officers to be discharged up to 90 days early if they were admitted to college, graduate or professional school.

During the year I was stationed at Fort Huachuca, Arizona, I took the Graduate Record Examination (GRE) at the University of Arizona in Tucson, about 60 miles from the post. I had decided to attend graduate school to earn a doctorate in political science. At the time, I was interested in African studies and applied to universities with reputable programs in this field: Boston University, Syracuse University and Northwestern University. I was admitted to Northwestern University and awarded a fellowship. Consequently, I received an honorable discharge and left Vietnam on September 14, 1970, so that I could enroll at Northwestern University fourteen days later on September 28, 1970.

## CHAPTER FIVE

# Graduate School

When I was drafted, Owens-Illinois was required to hire me once I completed my tour, even though I had been gone two years. The opportunity to exit early from Vietnam was the impetus to enroll in graduate school. But frankly, after getting acclimated to the academic environment, particularly the freedom and independence it provided, I began thinking about an academic career instead of returning to the private sector. This was quite a change since I was never keen on teaching. My intellectual curiosity was overwhelming however, and I felt compelled to explore and see where this might lead. To a degree, enrolling in graduate school was an extension of my deep desire to attend college. There was never a time in high school that I did not envision going to college. My inability to go to college straight out of Sacred Heart was disheartening. Although deflated, I never gave up on the dream of earning a college degree.

In part, I was inspired by family members and the many Black teachers, coaches and principals I had encountered as a student and basketball player at Sacred Heart. In addition, I had begun working for my Uncle Rufus Mayfield at Esquire Cleaners at age thirteen. His wife, Marion, was a teacher, and so were many of his customers. The bulk of Black professionals in Lake Charles when I was growing up were teachers. Most had nice homes, dressed well, drove nice cars and carried themselves with pride. However, I also had members of my family to look up to as role models.

The first college graduate in the family was my great-uncle, Roi Leland Hopkins, who finished at Texas College, a small Methodist institution in Tyler, Texas. Uncle Roi was my maternal grandmother's youngest brother. The next to finish college was my Aunt

Effie Lou Mayfield, who also graduated from Texas College. She was followed by my twin aunts, Janice and Janet Mayfield, who graduated from Xavier University. My oldest brother Thaddeus started Xavier in 1953, but left after a year to join the Air Force. My older sister, Lois, enrolled at Xavier in 1959, and she also left after her freshman year. I was determined to start and finish college and I would not let anything or anyone stand in my way. However, the decision to go to graduate school was different. I had not really thought about it until the draft interrupted my work at Owens-Illinois. My military experiences, the prevailing racial climate, and the optimism of new opportunities emerging from the civil rights movement all contributed to broadening my horizon about what I might do professionally and what it would take to get there.

## Life as a Graduate Student

In hindsight, I would have benefited from some professional counseling after leaving Vietnam and before starting a rigorous graduate school program. I plunged into my studies with focused attention. Always serious about my studies and everything else, I acquitted myself well in all of my courses. Never a strong student in math, I struggled in methods and statistics but I was not shy or diffident about seeking the help of a tutor. I earned top grades in political theory, urban politics and comparative politics. At the end of the academic year the political science faculty awarded me the Norman Wait Harris Fellowship as the outstanding first year student. There were twenty students in my class so I felt particularly honored to receive this recognition by the faculty. In addition, this was quite an affirmation, since there were times when I seriously considered dropping out.

Graduate school was very challenging but frankly, it was compounded by the fact that I was still dealing with some personal issues partly related to Vietnam and now from adjusting to Northwestern.

By personal issues I am referring to adjusting to civilian life, particularly graduate school after leaving Vietnam. I left Vietnam on September 14, 1970, and started graduate school fourteen days later. I barely had enough time to visit family in Louisiana, drop off my duffel bag and go to a place I had never been before. As well, I was leaving the jungles of Vietnam for a rigorous graduate program that I was anxious about.

I remember that when I arrived on the campus of Northwestern University I was startled whenever I heard a helicopter flying overhead. Students riding bicycles on sidewalks—which was fairly common at the time—was also unsettling and annoying. I was fearful that I might collide with one of them. A brief respite after Vietnam before starting graduate school might have been helpful but that was not possible under the conditions of my discharge.

In fall 1970 the department of political science admitted about 20 graduate students to its highly rigorous, research-oriented Ph.D. program. It included one Black female and four Black male students. Faculty were nice for the most part, but some seriously doubted that I and other Black students were worthy of the political science department—and they did not try to hide it. We were constantly under a looking glass having to prove ourselves at every turn. In addition, Black undergraduate students were struggling with similar issues and we felt obligated to act on their behalf. As well, there was a paucity of Black faculty and staff so we felt the need to weigh in on this issue as well.

Navigating graduate school can be daunting and admittedly, in retrospect, it is a wonder that many of us finished. Earning top grades, finding faculty who were willing to work with us, and selecting a dissertation topic they would support were not minor hurdles. Yet, at a time when we should have been concentrating on our studies we were drawn into larger concerns that were legitimate, but not necessarily within our purview alone to correct. We nonetheless made them our issues because we felt they could not be ignored and because we knew we were paving the way for others to follow.

By early spring 1971, we Black graduate students in the program were fed up. We drafted a position paper, signed it and requested a meeting with the entire political science faculty. It was a tense gathering but a necessary one. I was tasked with reading the statement excerpted below:

> These comments are made with genuine concern that the political science department address itself to the policy implications of future admission of Blacks into its Ph.D. program.... An amalgam of mixed reactions among students and faculty attended our arrival to the department..., faculty and students engaged us with suspicion and distance. Some decided that only the Ivy League grads among us were capable of academic success at Northwestern. One faculty member even intimated that indeed the department had yielded to tokenism as an expedient..., and if he had his way only Blacks with M.A.s, who had demonstrated mathematical skills would be admitted to the program.
>
> The message is this, "If this department is serious about the business of including Black people as an integral part of its Ph.D. program, its covert and sometimes explicit patronizing and condescending attitudes will have to cease. We didn't come here to be patronized, and neither did we come here to be run through the mill."
>
> Signed:
> Geneva G. Clemons
> S. Kofele-Kale
> Louis A. McCall
> George T. Mitchell
> Alvin J. Schexnider

In closing, we asked the department to explain "why, prior to this year, only Black students outside the continental United States were recruited, and why in the coming year the proportion of Blacks outside the country was so low?" We also asked the faculty to avoid insidious rumors, the prejudgment of capabilities and recognition that faculty and students were to some extent victims of culture shock.

Ultimately, during my graduate studies I got my bearings, sorted things out and forged ahead. At the same time, I learned to be clear about why I was in graduate school. That meant not getting so affected by racism that it impaired my ability to avail myself of a great learning experience that would prepare me for an exciting career.

The first year of graduate school was the most difficult; it was now behind me. Two or three students dropped out of the program, but I persisted and began my second year with confidence, encouraged substantially by being awarded the Norman Wait Harris Fellowship and the endorsement of faculty. I also had the financial support of the GI Bill that enabled me to enjoy a comfortable standard of living. Unlike many recently discharged veterans, I bought a used Volkswagen instead of a new car when I returned from the war. In the Army, I had developed the habit of saving, a practice that served me well as a graduate student and long afterward.

My second year of graduate school allowed more flexibility in selecting courses in political science, but also in areas outside the department. Soon after arriving at Northwestern, I met two Vietnam veterans, Johnny Butler and Charles Cole. Both were studying sociology and had struck up a relationship with the chairman of the department, Professor Charles C. Moskos. I was unfamiliar with his work but soon learned that Professor Moskos was a leading scholar in the area of civil-military relations. Moskos had a background similar to ours. He was drafted after graduating from Princeton University and served as an enlisted soldier in the Army. Moskos had traveled to Army units across the country interviewing soldiers for his acclaimed book *The American Enlisted Man*. He also collaborated closely with a fellow military sociologist at the University of Chicago, Morris Janowitz.

Charlie Moskos and I met during my second year of graduate school and shared our mutual interests in civil-military studies. He encouraged me to write about my Army experiences, particularly my time in Vietnam. Until meeting Charlie Moskos and learning more about his research, I had frankly not thought about the armed services as an area of intellectual interest and scholarly pursuit. After considerable reading and many conversations with Moskos and Butler, I began to think about civil-military relations as a serious matter of political inquiry. After all, Blacks had fought in every major battle this country has waged including the American Revolution. We were conscripted to fight in the Civil War and we demanded the right to fight in World War I. The participation of Blacks expanded in World War II, the Korean war and in Vietnam. Additionally, I recalled that my year at Fort Huachuca introduced me to a museum memorializing what was once an all–Black installation.

In 1917 Fort Huachuca had been commanded by Colonel Charles Young whose next promotion would have been brigadier general. The then segregated Army would not allow this to happen, purportedly because Young suffered from high blood pressure. To prove that the denial was based on race, Young rode a horse from Wilberforce, Ohio, to Washington. Upon arrival, he had his blood pressure checked. It was fine, but he was still denied a promotion and the Army subsequently retired Colonel Young. It was not until 1941 that Benjamin O. Davis, Sr., was awarded the one star of a brigadier general.[1] His son, Benjamin O. Davis, Jr., later led the Tuskegee Airmen and afterward rose to become the highest ranking Black officer in the United States Air Force. He retired as a Lieutenant General in 1967.[2]

With the encouragement of Professor Moskos, I began studying the role of Blacks in the armed services. My interest in the political implications of Blacks in the armed services was heightened by protests among Blacks about serving in the Vietnam War when rights were denied at home. Chief among the leaders of this protest movement was the heavyweight boxing champion Muhammad Ali, who was subsequently stripped of his title because he refused to submit to the draft.

During my second year of graduate study, I received a Ford Foundation Ethnic Studies Fellowship to continue my research in civil-military relations. The broad outlines of a research proposal had begun to emerge. Charlie Moskos agreed to chair my dissertation committee that was composed of three other members from the department of political science. This was an unusual arrangement, since typically only members of the department from which the degree is to be awarded serve as dissertation committee chair.

In my case, there was no one in my department with the expertise and commanding reputation of Charlie Moskos. Although there was grousing and at least one comment that "I had gone sociologist," the department approved Moskos to chair my committee.

After this hurdle was surmounted near the end of the year, Moskos informed me that he had been awarded a Fulbright Fellowship and would spend the 1973–74 academic year in Germany. I was totally unprepared for this. Basically, this meant that I would have to accelerate plans to conduct literature research, engage in original research including collecting data, regularly consult with my dissertation committee to seek approval, and finally write the dissertation and defend it before a faculty committee by summer 1973!

Moskos had built his reputation by interviewing enlisted men all over the world. He had great contacts with colonels and generals who respected him and his research, some of which informed policy they developed as battalion and brigade commanders. In order to pursue my research, I applied for and was awarded a Woodrow Wilson Dissertation Fellowship. This enabled me to go to Germany where I interviewed enlisted men for my dissertation, the subject of which was the political socialization of Black troops. I also interviewed Black soldiers at Fort Carson, Colorado, and Fort Polk, Louisiana, near my home in Lake Charles. I successfully defended my dissertation in August 1973, and earned a Ph.D. in political science.

When I decided to forgo returning to Owens-Illinois and to pursue graduate work instead, I had no idea where this would lead. I was convinced that it would create a brighter future, and it did. The first few years after completing graduate work, I continued to write about Blacks in the military and co-authored a book by the same title. It was published by the Brookings Institution in 1982. My research in this area also provided an opportunity in the summer of 1975 to work on the staff of the Defense Manpower Commission established by President Gerald Ford to study the All-Volunteer Force in the aftermath of the end of conscription.

## CHAPTER SIX

# A Reluctant Academic: 1973–1995

In August 1973 I successfully completed the requirements for the Ph.D. in political science at Northwestern University. It had been a grueling, intense, no-time-wasted experience that tested me severely: intellectually, physically and emotionally. I admit to being a bundle of nerves when I finished, but that did not matter. I did it, in spite of faculty members and fellow graduate students doubting my ability to complete it.

Throughout high school and college I never thought of myself as an outstanding student. I was smart, but many of my classmates were perhaps smarter. What made the difference for me was that I was disciplined and had developed a strong work ethic. In addition, I was never too proud to ask for help if I needed it. During the second half of my first year of graduate school I had doubts about whether to stay. I had a conversation with the only Black on the faculty in political science. He was having his own difficulties, I am sure, so he understood what I was going through and encouraged me to stay the course. I remember him saying, "If some of these dumb guys can get through the program you can too." Although I did not recognize it at the time, I was still feeling the aftereffects of Vietnam and all that I had experienced as a Black soldier. To a degree, writing the dissertation was cathartic, but as noted earlier I could have benefited from professional counseling (as did many Vietnam War veterans).

The political science department chair, David Minar, was a mentor and steadfast supporter. He felt I should interview at a Big Ten school where I could serve as a role model. I was saddened when he died unexpectedly during my second year. Professor Louis Masotti took up a strong interest in me and hired me during the summer of 1971 as an intern at the Northwestern University Center for Urban Affairs. Because of that experience, my first published article in the refereed *Journal of Urban Affairs Quarterly* came out in fall 1973.

Although the faculty urged me to apply for positions at White or majority universities, I decided to accept an appointment as an assistant professor of political science at Southern University in Baton Rouge. The department chair, Professor Jewel Prestage, was an alumna of the department and was one of a handful of Blacks in the country to earn a doctorate in political science. Dr. Prestage was active in the American Political Science Association and was a co-founder of the National Conference of Black Political Scientists (NCOBPS). The Southern University political science department had produced several outstanding men and women who earned the Ph.D. degree at leading research universities through the country. I felt I would be in good company and that this was a good place to launch my academic career. Additionally, Southern University in Baton Rouge, Louisiana, is just 140 miles from my home in Lake Charles. It would be great to be near family and friends, I reasoned.

As a graduate student, I was urged to conduct research and write at least one scholarly article each year. I explained to Dr. Prestage how important this was to me and requested some relief from the four courses each member of the faculty was required to teach each semester. She was very accommodating and allowed me to use a new and different textbook from the one the department had selected. Of course, this raised eyebrows among my faculty colleagues, some of whom felt I was getting special treatment—and frankly, I was, although that was not my intent.

Near the end of my first semester at Southern, I received a phone call from Louis Masotti, my mentor at Northwestern University informing me that the Syracuse University department of political science had a vacancy and was interested in me. He strongly urged me to apply. I told him I would consider it. This was not an easy decision. I liked my faculty colleagues and I liked being in Baton Rouge. Yet, I did not feel challenged at Southern and I had doubts about my ability to conduct research, write, and ultimately fulfill my potential there. The teaching load was oppressive and though I liked many of my students, the department simply did not provide what I was seeking at that point in my career.

My interview at Syracuse University resulted in a job offer, but with a modest salary reduction. My nine-month salary at Southern was $14,900; the most Syracuse was willing to pay was $14,000 for nine months. The department chair explained that I would have a lighter teaching load and I would be assigned a graduate teaching assistant. He also implied that because faculty positions at Syracuse University were coveted, due to their academic reputation, it was not difficult to recruit top talent. He was informing me of something that I would hear repeatedly throughout my academic career at majority schools, "you should be grateful to be here." Of course, I was not supposed to simply believe this; there was a corresponding expectation that I should behave this way also. That was never going to happen.

When I returned from Vietnam in 1970, instead of buying a new car, I found a used 1969 Volkswagen Beetle. It served me well throughout graduate school, easily managing Chicago's brutal winters. I had always wanted a sports car, so in April 1974, I bought a new Datsun (now Nissan) 260Z. This was the second series of a car that was introduced to the United States a few years earlier as the 240Z. I became enamored with this car while in Tokyo, Japan on R&R in 1970. There, it was known as the Fairlady.

The move to Syracuse gave me an opportunity to find out just how fast my car was. I joined the AAA Auto Club and got an itinerary that took me through Arkansas, Kansas, Ohio, and Pennsylvania before reaching New York. When I arrived in Syracuse, I stayed with a faculty member, Thomas Patterson, until I could find an apartment and accept delivery of my furniture from Baton Rouge. Tom was very kind and welcoming, and he did his best to help acclimate me to the department. I did not know it at the time, but not long after I began my sojourn at Syracuse University, I discovered that the dean of the Maxwell School of Citizenship and Public Affairs was the primary reason for my hiring.

Alan K. (Scotty) Campbell was dean of the Maxwell School at Syracuse University when I was recruited. The Maxwell School was perhaps best known for its public administration program. The Maxwell MPA (Master of Public Administration) degree was highly respected and widely known for producing outstanding and highly sought-after city managers. The MPA was arguably one of the best known degree programs at Syracuse University and the Maxwell School enjoyed a vaunted status within it. The school also contained departments of urban and regional planning, geography, and political science. I believe Scotty Campbell was more interested in recruiting a Black political scientist than the department itself was. I am fairly certain that Campbell and Masotti were professional colleagues and that Scotty sought help in integrating the political science faculty.

As part of the recruitment and hiring process, I had to make a presentation on my research interests to the political science department faculty. I did not feel particularly good about their interest in my research or me. After my forum, I was invited to a reception with three other recruits in order to mingle and socialize with department faculty. This was an odd arrangement knowing that only one of us would be hired. As it turned out, assistant professor positions were offered to Kenneth Auerbach and me. Ken's area was international relations; mine was metropolitan politics. Dean Campbell became involved in the Jimmy Carter presidential election campaign in 1976. When Carter won, Campbell was named chairman of the United States Civil Service Commission, later renamed the Office of Personnel Management. Campbell's leaving meant that I no longer had a mentor and supporter in a department that did not want me in the first place although I did not realize it at the time.

In summer 1976, I was asked to interview for a faculty position at the Federal Executive Institute (FEI) in Charlottesville, Virginia.

The principal advocate for recruiting me was Dr. Jeffalyn Johnson, who held a doctorate in public administration from the University of Southern California. Frankly, I had not heard of FEI and neither did I appreciate its reputation as the federal government's premier executive development and management training center for the women and men who ran the federal government. Consequently, although I made a favorable impression on the faculty, I demurred and decided to remain at Syracuse University. It did not take long for me to realize that I had made a major miscalculation.

I never felt welcome in the department of political science. Several of my faculty colleagues were condescending and my research interests were not respected. Equally important, although I did not understand it at the time, the long grey winters with little or no sunshine had begun to take a toll. Seasonal Affective Disorder, or what is commonly referred to as SAD by psychologists, is what I experienced. I recall lecturing in Maxwell one spring morning in April when the sun broke through the glass windows in the ceiling. It was almost like I had died and gone to heaven. That feeling stayed with me for months. Later it became crystal clear that I had made a mistake in spurning the offer to join the faculty of the Federal Executive Institute (FEI).

While I dithered about accepting FEI's offer, Walter Broadnax who had just completed a Ph.D. in public administration at Maxwell was hired. Walter's leaving meant that I was losing a friend and colleague where the number of Black faculty and staff was minuscule. I began to rethink my decision and contacted FEI about joining the faculty there. In all candor, I had doubts about FEI having two Blacks on its faculty. In most instances, organizations, whether public, private or third sector, behaved as though one Black hire was adequate. At the time, FEI had about fifteen faculty members. Dr. Johnson had decided to leave to work with the Carter administration transition team, thereby creating a vacancy which made my hiring possible.

Not long after I arrived at FEI, Scotty Campbell and I crossed paths again when as chairman of the U.S. Civil Service Commission he visited FEI. As I reflect on my career, I am convinced that my two and one-half years at FEI had perhaps the greatest impact on me, both personally and professionally, that I have experienced anywhere. Lessons I learned about my profession and tips for success along with friendships I made at FEI have been beneficial in ways I could never have imagined. In addition to meeting and interacting with some of the nation's outstanding scholars and professional public managers, I learned to appreciate the importance of maintaining balance in one's personal and professional life; the importance of stress management and time management; an appreciation for executive education and professional development; and the enormous value of a simple instrument like the Myers-Briggs Type Indicator, an invaluable tool for leadership development. In no uncertain terms, my brief tenure at FEI has served me enormously well. Additionally, while in Charlottesville, I met a very special woman who would become my life partner.

I resigned from Syracuse University in December 1976. When I informed the department chairman, Ronald McDonald, who was never supportive, he was not at all disappointed and said he would not stand in my way. I was not about to let anything prevent me from leaving a very unhappy situation.

## *Leadership and Public Service*

From the standpoint of personal and professional development, nothing influenced the trajectory of my academic path more than my two and one-half years at the Federal Executive Institute (FEI), a residential executive education program for the country's top career professionals in Charlottesville, Virginia. The FEI shaped my career like no other job before or since. It was an epiphany of sorts. As a trained political scientist, I had an understanding of politics or what Robert Dahl characterized as the study of "who gets what, when, and how," but I had little knowledge about the administration or management of political decision-making and the distribution of political rewards.

The FEI opened my eyes to the difference between leadership and management. At the FEI, I discovered a vast literature about leadership—studying whether leaders are born or made, how leaders are developed, and how people find themselves in leadership positions in the first place. When the FEI opened its doors in 1968, its programs were limited to approximately 8300 "super-grades," the highest levels of career federal civil servants. As its founding director Frank Sherwood explained, over time the FEI's mission and focus changed from an exclusive focus on top leadership to a more expanded notion. In a thoughtful history of the FEI Sherwood observed that "The concern at today's FEI is not with the very top, but with those layers of managers charged more directly with seeing that things work."[1]

At the FEI, I learned that individuals rise to leadership positions based on some demonstrated technical expertise. For example, a highly competent teacher may become a supervisor and eventually a principal. An outstanding department chair may become dean. Continued progression to higher levels of leadership requires a lot more than technical know-how. What intrigued me most about the FEI was its emphasis on what are today called, "soft skills: organization development, team-building, time management, and stress management."

Prior to the Federal Executive Institute I honestly but wrongly believed that I could advance my career by being smart, hardworking, focused, and effective. Also, I was narrowly focused on politics and government, rather than leadership and management. I had little to no understanding of the critical importance of soft skills and emotional intelligence. My daily interactions with the federal executives who came to the FEI for one of its one-month or two month programs provided a rich laboratory, a learning community, where if I listened and observed, I could soak up information simply by being in the presence of women and men who ran every federal agency from the National Institutes of Health to the Nuclear Regulatory Commission and the United States Secret Service. My time at the FEI set the stage for honing a career path at Virginia Commonwealth University (VCU) and afforded an opportunity to apply what I had learned there in a more traditional academic setting. An added bonus to my faculty appointment was meeting my future life partner, Virginia Reeves, who was a graduate psychology student at the University of Virginia. One of the things I learned at the FEI was the importance of seeking balance between one's personal and professional life. Charlottesville was a stuffy college town where nearly every aspect of social life swirled around the university. Meeting and marrying Virginia filled a huge void and helped me focus on developing a personal life that was not consumed by work and career as the FEI sought to instill in its executive education programs.

I admit to some reticence about returning to the South after several years at Northwestern and Syracuse. I knew little about the Federal Executive Institute, and even less about Charlottesville, Virginia. My adventuresome, inquisitive nature prevailed however, and I plunged into a totally new environment. The FEI faculty was small, about fifteen in number with eight or ten administrative or support staff. Faculty spent a lot of time together and were on a first name basis with one another, including the federal executives, or "execs" as we called them.

The execs were highly accomplished and many had advanced degrees such as physicians from the National Institutes of Health or lawyers from the National Labor Relations Board. They also included research scientists, accountants, engineers, and physicists representing every federal agency.

These were men and women who ran the United States government. A new or re-elected president takes office every four years. In our system of government, the Executive Branch, that is, those in charge of the federal agencies, continue in their positions with the exception of the president's cabinet. They and key deputies are selected by the president, along with their top subordinates (for example, deputy secretary, undersecretary and deputy assistant secretary, etc.).

When I arrived in Charlottesville in January 1977, there was two feet of snow on the ground, but the sun was shining! I knew immediately that I had made the right decision to move, even though resigning a faculty position in mid-year was unusual. Patience has never been my strong suit; however, I did not second guess the need for change. Again, returning to the South dredged up old fears about how a Black man with a Ph.D. would be received in Thomas Jefferson's hometown.

When I was shown my office the nameplate on the door read "Al Schexnider" while my colleagues had their full names written as Roger P. Smith, John E. Jones and David W. Baker, etc. Immediately, I interpreted this as a racial slight even though I was accustomed to being called Al since graduate school. Nonetheless, I was not about to allow anyone to take me for granted. I requested a new nameplate that read "Alvin J. Schexnider" and asked everyone to call me Alvin.

Charlottesville, Virginia, in 1977 was not an easy place to meet new people and develop friends, particularly in the Black community. The Black middle class was small and local social groups were few and not easy to join. There were not many Black faculty at the University of Virginia; however, I was fortunate to meet one of the handful there and a genuinely good guy, Dr. William (Bill) Harris, professor of urban and regional planning. Bill was also the founding dean of UVA's Department of Afro-American Affairs. Under his leadership, the university created a program that consistently leads the nation in the number of African Americans who graduate at rates comparable to that of White students. That UVA has maintained this distinction is due in no small part to the genius, commitment and hard work of Dr. Harris and his colleagues. Bill is special for another reason and that is because of his role in introducing me to the woman who would become my partner for life.

In mid–September 1977 I vacationed in Costa del Sol, Spain. It was my first and only excursion to that part of Europe. When I returned, I attended a reception that Dr. Harris and his staff hosted for Black faculty and staff at UVA. It was at that reception that I met Virginia Young Reeves, the love of my life, a doctoral student from Salem, Virginia. It was also the start of a romance that led to a marriage proposal four months later.

## Virginia Commonwealth University (VCU)

On July 1, 1978, Virginia and I were married in her hometown Salem, Virginia. My family traveled from Louisiana, Texas, and New York to join us in the joyous occasion. After a honeymoon in St. Maarten, Dutch West Indies, we settled into a townhouse at 65 Georgetown Green in Charlottesville. Virginia continued her graduate studies at the University of Virginia while I continued my work at the Federal Executive Institute.

One year later in July 1979, I arrived at VCU in Richmond, Virginia, as an associate professor and associate dean of the School of Community Services. I had been recruited by the School's dean, Laurin Henry, a noted expert on presidential transitions with a Ph.D. in political science from the University of Chicago. Laurin was on the faculty of UVA's Department of Government and Foreign Affairs. He also taught a course on the American presidency at the Federal Executive Institute where our paths first crossed. Neither of us liked the name of the school, which was an amalgam of professional degree programs including urban and regional planning, public administration, criminal justice and rehabilitation counseling, but the politics at the time precluded a name change more reflective of our mission and professional aspirations. Years later, after Laurin and I left VCU, the school was reincarnated as the L. Douglas Wilder School of Government and Public Affairs. Laurin encouraged me to continue research and publishing while carrying out academic administrative duties. Consequently, it was at VCU where I earned tenure as an associate professor.

Working at the FEI was an invaluable learning experience, one that shaped my career in profound and lasting ways. I thought I understood the federal government and the inner workings of bureaucracy but the FEI provided insights that I could never have imagined. It also taught me lessons about leadership, executive development and strategies to create and sustain a career path. Leaving FEI for VCU was also positive because as young Black professionals, Virginia and I felt a huge void in our social lives. The Charlottesville Black middle class was small, many activities centered around the University of Virginia and despite its prestige and reputation, the city was viewed by Blacks we knew as racist and frozen in a time warp. Frankly, we could not wait to escape and get on with our lives in a bigger city that offered a lot more exciting things to do than we found in Charlottesville.

When I arrived at VCU it was mainly a commuter school. Most students lived off-campus because there were few dormitories and many were adults who held full-time jobs. I liked the fact that VCU prided itself on being affordable and accessible. Given my own background and having attended a public university, these values resonated strongly and I was happy to be a part of an institution that extended opportunities to students, many of whom were the first in their family to attend college. Friends and former colleagues asked why I passed up opportunities to work at better known universities but I had no doubt that VCU was where I could both pursue a career and help students achieve their goals. In addition, as the state capital, Richmond was a rich laboratory for any student of politics and public affairs, and its social and professional environment was one that Virginia and I found very attractive and responsive to our expectations.

We felt very much at home in Richmond despite its insular, standoffish ways. It was an exciting place even if it was the former capital of the Confederacy. At the time there were two daily newspapers, the *Richmond Times-Dispatch* and the *Richmond News Leader*, the former in the morning and the latter in the afternoon. Something newsworthy happened all the time and I could not get enough.

I made it a priority to meet Black members of the Richmond City Council and Black legislators in the Virginia General Assembly, one of whom was extraordinarily impressive and later became the first Black elected to statewide office as lieutenant governor and later as governor of the Commonwealth of Virginia. L. Douglas Wilder had been elected to the Virginia Senate in 1969 and thereafter blazed a trail as an effective legislator and political strategist creating a legacy that remains unmatched.

When I arrived at VCU in 1979 it was still in the throes of a transformation from two institutions to a single university with a distinct identity. Virginia Commonwealth University was created by an act of the legislature in 1968 consolidating the Richmond Professional Institute with the Medical College of Virginia. Eleven years later it was still two institutions, two operating units and two organizational cultures. Change comes slowly as anyone bold enough to try to lead change quickly learns. There were times at VCU when I chafed at the slow pace of change and tried to hasten things along. I was told that I came across as a "young man in a hurry" who was "too direct" and that I needed to understand "the Virginia way." One day I found a card on my desk, sent anonymously, of course. It read, "You must have been a hemorrhoid because you are a pain in the ass." I laughed. I wish that whoever left the card would have had the courage to confront me directly. Few are willing to do so.

After two and a half years in Charlottesville, I was eager to get involved in public affairs in Richmond, Virginia's capital. Virginia Commonwealth's Academic Campus, as it was then called, was located in the Fan District, clearly within the city and a stone's throw from City Hall, the Virginia General Assembly, and numerous state and local agencies situated nearby. I was excited about the new opportunities for civic engagement and, thankfully, Laurin recognized the possibilities for building the school and encouraged me to cultivate relationships with state and local officials. It helped that Richmond's city manager at the time, Manuel Deese, was a friend whom I had known since the 1960s. Deese respected me and opened doors that proved helpful to VCU and the academic programs in our school.

Although Dean Henry and I did not set out to be the face of VCU, because of our school's degree programs, particularly public administration and urban and regional planning, perhaps more than any other academic unit, we attained a high degree of visibility. After some politicking we succeeded in changing the name to the School of Community and Public Affairs so as not to confuse it with public works and refuse collection.

By the early 1980s our school was increasingly called upon to work with state and local agencies in addressing perplexing urban problems. Laurin and I recognized that in advancing the school's agenda, we were simultaneously fulfilling the mission of a major public urban university even if the folk at the top did not understand or appreciate it. We knew that we were simply satisfying roles expected of schools of public affairs like ours across the country. In point of fact, Laurin Henry was one of the founders of the National Association of Schools of Public Affairs and Administration (NASPAA). Yet in its infancy VCU had not developed an appreciation for what a school like ours could do for capacity-building as well as burnishing the university's academic reputation. We knew, however, that we were laying the groundwork for something much bigger than our school, and that is why we are so proud of the Wilder School of Government and Public Affairs.

The School of Community and Public Affairs was helpful in another way that has not been fully appreciated. One of the school's major degree programs was the Department of Public Administration, which offered a Master of Public Administration (MPA) degree, the pedigree for individuals seeking executive positions in local (city manager, for example) or state government (director of public safety, for example).

Our FEI colleague, Dr. Chong M. Pak, had been the Federal Executive Institute's Associate Director before being appointed Director of Personnel and Training by Governor Gerald Baliles. As the Commonwealth of Virginia's chief human resources officer, Dr. Pak created the Virginia Executive Institute (VEI) which was modeled on the Federal Executive Institute. Thanks to Dr. Pak, for several years I taught regularly in the VEI, which has had a major impact on professionalizing the state's senior executive workforce. The school's MPA degree program, coupled with its ties to the VEI, contributed substantially to improving the quality of the state's employees while also enhancing VCU's image in the state and the region. Two separate but consequential decisions helped to accelerate my path toward more focused involvement in leadership and civic engagement in Richmond. VCU was the principal beneficiary, since I received no monetary or direct material inducement because of my involvement.

## Leadership Metro Richmond (LMR)

In the summer of 1980, the Richmond Chamber of Commerce launched Leadership Metro Richmond. I was selected to join the original class composed of emerging leaders representing business, government, medicine, banking, law, higher education and non-profit organizations. LMR enabled me to get to know Richmond quicker and better and to network with other young professionals. I was subsequently asked to serve on a number of public, private and non-profit boards and committees. Richmond's first Black city manager, Manuel Deese, was enormously helpful in opening several doors for me. I am forever grateful for his friendship and support.

## Commission on Virginia's Future

The second major opportunity to further my career aspirations and to be helpful to VCU came from my appointment to Virginia's Commission on Virginia's Future. Created by Governor Chuck Robb in 1982, the Commission was charged with taking a long-range examination of all aspects of Virginia's government, its economy, and its business prospects, and recommending actions to improve the quality of life for all Virginians. The Commission was chaired by former U.S. Senator William B. Spong and its membership included key members of Governor Robb's cabinet along with the speaker of the house, the senate majority leader, and prominent legislators, business executives, and civic leaders. I was careful not to rely upon my personal and professional connections to intentionally advance my career at VCU. It was important to me that I achieve professional goals on the basis of merit and not politics. I was purposeful to a fault in doing my job and fulfilling responsibilities and duties, first as associate dean of the school and later as associate vice president for academic affairs and vice provost for undergraduate studies.

Universities and colleges operate to varying degrees on the principle of shared governance. One way that faculty and staff meet the expectation of shared governance is by spending a considerable amount of time on committees. As an academic administrator, I was no exception. It was important that I pay attention to my day job and not allow external activities to get in the way.

During the period 1987 to 1995, I served as associate vice president for academic affairs and later vice provost for undergraduate studies. A major part of my responsibilities entailed chairing various committees. Some of the committees I chaired were confined to the Academic (now Monroe Park) Campus. The Academic Support Coordinating Committee and the Doctor of Public Administration (DPA) Program Committee; for example, had a limited purview. Two that I chaired, the University Curriculum Committee and the University Calendar Committee, covered both campuses and sometimes proved difficult. Even in the 1980s and 1990s, VCU was still grappling with two distinct organizational cultures and two different ways of doing business. On certain matters there might be conformity, but often there were differences. I had learned at FEI that the incumbent makes the role and without prodding or explicit direction and support from the president or the provost to whom I reported, I decided to do my part to foster the notion of a singular university by extending the reach of committees I chaired to the MCV Campus. This did not engender warm and fuzzy feelings from my colleagues on the MCV Campus who served on committees that I believed should be truly university-wide in scope and oversight. The Curriculum Committee in particular is one where I felt strongly that we should seek broad participation and consensus. Allied health programs like nursing, medicine, and dentistry for example, needed to consult and collaborate with faculty on both campuses to ensure student success. I pushed ahead with this approach, but it did not make me popular with faculty and deans on the MCV Campus. I am certain that several colleagues expressed their displeasure to top leadership. I was not deterred because I believed in what I was doing and that my actions were in the long-term interest of creating a unified university.

The other committee that I chaired that enjoyed a university-wide focus was the University Calendar Committee. Arguably, it was among the most important committees since it determined the academic schedule and which holidays were to be celebrated throughout the school year. I understood its power and was not afraid to wield it.

For several years, Senator L. Douglas Wilder sought recognition of Martin Luther King Day as an official state holiday. By the early 1980s, seventeen states had created a King holiday and in 1983, after a long national campaign led by Black elected officials, athletes and entertainers, it was designated a federal holiday. Senator Wilder was steadfast in the pursuit of a King holiday in Virginia, and in 1984, the Virginia General Assembly enacted a compromise. Rather than a separate holiday for Dr. King, it would now be celebrated as Lee-Jackson-King Day. This was not ideal, but a victory nonetheless. Given the tenor of the times in Virginia, this was no mean feat and Senator Wilder deserves enormous credit for his astute leadership and relentless pursuit without which legislative approval of the King Holiday would never have occurred.

---

While attending to my duties at VCU, I kept a steady eye on the Virginia General Assembly; hence, when it approved the MLK holiday, I looked for the opportunity to get it on the official University Schedule. As committee chair in 1992, I was able to secure recognition of Lee-Jackson-King on VCU's official University Holiday Schedule. Previously, it had been a flexible holiday allowing employees to choose from among two state holidays. Now, it was a fixed holiday observed by all employees. This approval by the calendar committee made VCU the first public university to recognize Martin Luther King's birthday.

The joint Lee-Jackson-King Day remained in effect until 2000, when the holidays were separated, thereby according Dr. King the respect and honor he rightly deserved. It was L. Douglas Wilder who laid the groundwork, cleared the path and set the stage not only for a stand-alone King holiday, but for bringing the Commonwealth of Virginia into a new progressive era for all its citizens.

For my role in getting the King holiday on VCU's official schedule I incurred the wrath of the Sons of Confederate Virginians who regularly wrote letters of protest each year, a practice that continued until I resigned in December 1995 to accept the position of chancellor of Winston-Salem State University.

## The Black Education Association (BEA)

Being a Black man is not something that can be dispensed with even if one desires to. The eminent historian W.E.B. DuBois has described this most eloquently in his writings, particularly, the *Souls of Black Folk*. While I have always embraced who I am and what I stand for, I have not allowed my identity to temper my goals and ambitions, either. As a senior administrator at VCU, and everywhere I worked, it was important to me that I was involved, supported the interests and aspirations of Black faculty and staff, and women and minority faculty as well. The Black Education Association or BEA

From left to right are the author; Richmond, Virginia businessman and civic leader S. Buford Scott; and noted civil rights lawyer Oliver W. Hill, at a civic event in Richmond, Virginia (author's collection).

was the main vehicle at VCU for advancing these pursuits. Although mindful of my duties and responsibilities as an officer of the university, I would not ignore, compromise or narrowly construe my role to the detriment of Black students, faculty or staff. I was always under a looking glass and I accepted the scrutiny as part of the territory.

In 1984 Laurin Henry called me into his office and stated that we were facing a tight budget and that he had to develop an alternative scenario that would result in a staff reduction. He informed me that my position was one that he could sacrifice if he had to cut the budget. This was a surprise and a disappointment but rather than curse the night I began exploring opportunities. As a tenured associate professor, I could have stayed in a teaching role. After serving five years as associate dean, however, I discovered a passion for administration and academic leadership and I wanted to continue on that career path. I had begun reading books and articles on leadership, such as *Academic Strategy, In Search of Excellence,* and Benjamin Mays' *Born to Rebel,* prompting thoughts about more challenging assignments.

Leaving VCU and Richmond was not in my plans at this stage of my career but I was determined to play the hand that had been dealt me. Our son, Alvin, was not yet two years old and we had developed lasting friendships in Richmond. My family in Lake Charles could not understand why I was moving again and I did not try to explain. No one in my family had ever had a career in higher education. The concept of an academic nomad was foreign to them as was tenure. My career developed during an era when faculty advanced their career by moving to another college or university, usually with the lure of a promotion, more money, better research facilities, or even faculty camaraderie. This changed significantly with the advent of two-career families where both spouses had to be professionally accommodated. Thankfully, Virginia and I agreed on the importance of deferring her professional aspirations in favor of child rearing until Alvin and Elena entered pre-school. We have never regretted that decision although it came with sacrifices.

After careful explorations in 1987 I accepted a job as assistant vice chancellor for academic affairs at the University of North Carolina Greensboro (UNCG). This was a wonderful opportunity to work at a great institution that was part of the University of North Carolina (UNC) System. The UNCG was located in Greensboro, North Carolina, a nice city with attractive neighborhoods. North Carolina A&T State University was also located there, and unlike Charlottesville, Greensboro had a thriving Black middle class. My specific duties there included creating an enrollment management unit within the office of the vice chancellor for academic affairs. I viewed this as a great opportunity to apply what I had learned at VCU, as well as from my years at FEI. At the time, UNCG was approaching 10,000 students. My responsibilities were university-wide, and I was able to successfully launch this new venture with substantial help from a seasoned admissions officer, Charles Rickard, whom I recruited from the University of Michigan–Flint. We worked closely together in building an effective enrollment strategy and program that helped to transform UNCG from the former Women's College of the University of North Carolina to a respected comprehensive liberal arts institution with solid undergraduate and graduate programs.

Our daughter, Elena, was born in Greensboro. For the most part, we were happy there. It was a nice community and we were actually closer to Salem, Virginia, which enabled regular visits to Virginia's parents. Richmond still had a hold on me, however. I missed connections to Richmond politics and social life and we missed our friends. VCU remained attractive and the city and the university together were unbeatable, so when the opportunity in 1987 to return as Associate Vice President for Academic Affairs presented itself, I did not hesitate.

## *The Return to VCU*

Previously, we lived in south Richmond; this time we found a lovely house in an attractive neighborhood just north of the city in Henrico County. Chickahominy Bluffs was a very nice development composed of middle-class professionals. It was integrated with good schools and parks and getting into town was relatively easy. Virginia considered the house we bought her dream home. I liked it too, although I did not like the fact that it was all-electric. We had lots of trees and when major storms toppled power lines we lost electricity for an extended period. By then, I had learned that "a happy wife is a happy life" and whatever concerns I had about an all-electric house evaporated.

Returning to VCU was a fascinating study of personal achievement but also excitement at the prospect of having found a place where my family could call home. Some would argue that it is

**At home with family on Easter Sunday in Richmond, Virginia, ca. 1991** (author's collection).

never a good idea to travel the same road twice, a view an uncle had expressed in my youth. Frankly, I was happy to be back. In fact, I planned to stay in Richmond a very long time. Even though I had begun to think about pursuing a presidency at a Black college it was my intention to stay at VCU for the foreseeable future.

Another reason for returning to VCU was I wanted to be a part of helping to elect L. Douglas Wilder to the state's highest office. I was at the University of North Carolina Greensboro when he was elected lieutenant governor and I did not want to miss the opportunity to help him advance to governor. Even while away, I kept in touch with him, contributed to his campaign and resumed support when I returned.

I had followed Doug Wilder's political career since arriving in Charlottesville in 1977. I read the *Washington Post* and the *Richmond*

*Times-Dispatch* daily. He could be counted on to provide leadership on matters pertaining to civil rights, but also on vital issues that benefited all Virginians. At the time he was the lone Black senator in the Virginia General Assembly's upper chamber that had forty members. Rarely did Senator Wilder disappoint. He understood the Senate's rules and procedures, and it did not hurt that he was a successful criminal defense lawyer. Wilder possessed a keen intellect and he was an excellent orator, always quick to display a knack for street smarts and the art of political theater. In many ways, he reminded me of Congressman Adam Clayton Powell. In Virginia, that was saying a lot. Doug Wilder was daring, even brazen, some might say. From the time he entered the Virginia Senate, he proclaimed that he sought change to improve the lives of all Virginians. In the course of his long career that is exactly what he did. Wilder was called many things, but benchwarmer was never one of them.

When Lt. Governor Wilder launched his campaign for Governor, I was ready to support him financially and in any other way. I had access to polling data from VCU's public policy center whose pollster Dr. Scott Keeter was one of the best. Scott later left VCU to join the Pew Center. Scott provided polling data on the gubernatorial race that I delivered promptly to Mark Warner, Wilder's campaign manager, whose office was near VCU's Academic Campus across from Monroe Park, one block from my office in Ginter Hall.

As much as anything I have accomplished in a career that spanned five decades, returning to Richmond and having a small role in helping elect L. Douglas Wilder as governor stands as a supreme highlight. Three decades later, today's Millennials may find it hard to understand why this was such a big deal. Many of their generation seemingly cannot wrap their minds around the evils of segregation, the dominance of the Byrd Machine, and the decision to close schools in the name of massive resistance rather than desegregate public, taxpayer-supported education. I have characterized Wilder's election as the greatest political feat of the twentieth century. The election of Edward Brooke as United States Senator from

Massachusetts and the election of Carl Stokes, Richard Hatcher, Kenneth Gibson and Coleman Young as mayors of Cleveland (Ohio), Gary (Indiana), Newark (New Jersey), and Detroit (Michigan), respectively, although significant, do not compare with the election of L. Douglas Wilder as governor of the Commonwealth of Virginia. When he assumed office in 1990, it was the culmination of a long journey that fulfilled dreams and unlocked doors that had been closed for centuries. As a student of politics and government, I had a ringside seat that was incomparable.

Three years after I returned VCU President Edmund Ackell retired and was succeeded by Dr. Eugene Trani in 1990. His appointment as president of VCU coincided with the onset of Governor Wilder's administration. In fact, Governor Wilder was the keynote speaker at President Trani's inauguration. Although for several years I had known Governor Wilder and several other key political figures both Black and White, not once did I use political connections to influence my professional career at VCU or any other university for that matter. It was important that I earn my spurs and the respect of my peers and colleagues. This did not prevent me from using what little outside influence I enjoyed to help VCU, however.

Prior to the arrival of President Trani, I was aware of and in some ways tied to the inner workings of local and state government. Richmond's city manager, Manuel Deese, was a friend I had known since the 1960s. When he retired to accept a position in the private sector, he was replaced by another friend and former college classmate, Robert Bobb. Consequently my local government ties continued.

In the early 1980s, I had staffed a local government commission that studied ways to improve operational efficiencies and effectiveness and I had received several gubernatorial appointments. Although I never sought to usurp anyone's authority, my position as associate vice president for academic affairs provided a platform to speak on matters pertaining to my position. Frankly, I saw myself filling a void; few VCU senior administrators seemed willing or able to connect with civic leaders, particularly Black leaders many of whom were emerging in key leadership positions in local and state government. Also, I did not hesitate to use my position to speak out on matters pertaining to race and educational opportunity, never to impugn or demean anyone but simply to affirm VCU's commitment. My supervisor, Provost Charles Ruch, understood and supported what I was trying to do inside VCU and in the larger community, although some did not.

Nonetheless, there were times when I was perceived with disfavor by some VCU colleagues. My formal, business-like leadership style didn't help soften that perception. I was constantly aware of the expectation of some Whites that Blacks were expected to perform and entertain irrespective of their profession or calling. Without uttering a word, my professional demeanor conveyed a seriousness of purpose in all things, large and small. I was aware of those who felt threatened by me but tried nonetheless to work with everyone.

In 1991 I was promoted to vice provost for undergraduate studies. This strengthened my role as associate vice president and it signaled recognition of my leadership potential. I was appreciative of the promotion, but it seemed at every turn I was expected to express my gratitude. I could never bring myself to do this, which likely made me appear ungrateful. This is a prime example of what my friend and former colleague Dr. Jackson Wright describes as reassuring Whites that "I'm so grateful to be here." My experience in this regard is not unique. Rather, it is a familiar refrain recounted by Black faculty staff and students at colleges and universities throughout the country.

My inability to express gratitude or show that I am "so happy to be here" was viewed by some as arrogance. I suspect some were whispering that I did not deserve the promotion, or they did not like my leadership style, or my memoranda were too blunt and direct. Nothing was going to stop me from being who I am so I simply ignored my detractors.

In hindsight, I could have benefited from a better appreciation of the value of emotional intelligence. Although I was careful not to become typecast as the angry Black man, I have no doubt that some viewed me that way and were afraid or resentful. I am certain there were those who simply could not accept a Black man in a leadership role, no matter how competent he was. I could not nor would I change my persona. I don't doubt that there were occasions when I could have softened the tone or been more strategic in what I said and how I implemented certain decisions. One of the travails of working in challenging situations is that it often requires being tactful and wise. Managing under these circumstances is often delicate. The masterful uses of emotional intelligence and soft skills can make a huge difference in leader's effectiveness.

Although FEI taught me the value of interpersonal skills for effective leadership, admittedly, in retrospect, it is clear that it took a while for me to fully grasp its importance. VCU is where I began to build a career as an academic administrator. Though there were times when I was not always approachable, and while I considered myself competent, in some things, I was inexperienced and unwilling to acknowledge room for growth.

In retrospect, I believed if I did my job well that was all that was required for success. I did not go out of my way to socialize or interact with colleagues I felt harbored views different from mine, particularly on matters of race. I was judgmental and dismissive of anyone who did not fit a certain mold. Sometimes colleagues made comments that were offensive or insensitive because of ignorance. Often I was exhausted and tired of always having to educate and explain matters pertaining to race. There were countless teachable moments, so to speak, but I had no interest in trying to help Whites better understand Black people. The onus to improve relations was always on us, a burden that was both unfair and unrealistic.

My return to VCU helped me to focus on being intentional about softening my approach and determined to build relationships with colleagues in and outside of the university community. This strategy seemed to work. In time, one colleague, a senior administrator whom

I knew but did not particularly like, shared with me over lunch that I was not the pompous arrogant guy he previously perceived me to be. I was tempted to say, but did not, that I no longer felt he was a backward, pretentious conservative from West Virginia. VCU gave me an opportunity to grow and develop personally and professionally. Its cautious, conservative ways mirrored Richmond and the Commonwealth of Virginia. I probably was "a young man in a hurry," as one colleague described me, but that did not mean I should have been penalized.

The prevailing attitude was that it was okay for young White professionals to be ambitious, but this did not apply to young Black professionals. Put another way, it is okay for Whites to be self-confident, but self-confidence in Blacks is seen as arrogance. I did not like, nor would I accept, this double standard, but I became more aware of how it impacted work relationships and ultimately my career. I refused to change who I was and what I believed; instead, I became more mindful and self-aware. The literature of emotional intelligence was sparse at that time, but through my interest in professional development and executive education, I acquired a better appreciation of how to deal with various personalities in the workplace and how to manage my own career in the process.

There were times when I stumbled despite my best efforts. Chairing the university's undergraduate curriculum committee was one of them. For one, I was aware of the tensions between the two campuses, but I failed to recognize the depth of the antipathy. Of course, I knew the history of the university and the resentments that followed what I characterized as a shotgun marriage. I viewed the curriculum committee as an opportunity to unify two campuses that three decades later were still separate operating units for the most part. I believed being intentional about building a collaborative relationship was the right thing to do. The committee's faculty representatives on the MCV Campus were generally unenthusiastic about this approach but went along with it. I have no doubt that this made me unpopular if not a pariah in that space.

I was clearly in uncharted waters. Often, I was alone in pushing the envelope toward building an inclusive organizational culture in order to achieve its potential as an urban, comprehensive research university. That is not to say others in administration did not share my enthusiasm or commitment to diversity, but perhaps they did not exhibit a passion for it. On separate occasions, I had verbal clashes with the medical school dean, the dental school dean and the dean of the nursing school. I knew that I was the topic of discussion, or more precisely consternation on the MCV Campus especially, but I ignored the naysayers and persisted.

Virginia Commonwealth University was essentially a university in name only. In order to realize its full potential, it had to begin acting like one, not two distinct organizations with duplicate, parallel systems that often did not communicate with one another. As a student of public management, I felt compelled to do my small part to improve the organization, but in point of fact, this was not a shared goal. I was aware that I had stepped on big toes, and it was only a matter of time before I would have to account for my actions, however, well-intended.

## *The Resignation of the Provost and Vice President for Academic Affairs*

Two years and ten months after Eugene Trani's arrival, my supervisor, Charles Ruch, announced that he was leaving to become president of Boise State University in Idaho. It was understandable and expected from the start that President Trani would want his own leadership team. I have no doubt that Provost Chuck Ruch understood this as well. His departure sparked speculation about who would be appointed provost. Reporting to Chuck Ruch were two African Americans, my friend and colleague, Dr. Grace Harris, vice provost for continuing studies, and I in the role of vice provost for undergraduate studies and associate vice president for academic affairs. Both of us held major leadership positions at VCU. Grace Harris was several years my senior, had been at VCU much longer than I had and was widely admired and respected in the larger Richmond community where she had lived since launching her career as a social worker in the 1950s. She had also served as dean of VCU's School of Social Work before being elevated to vice provost by President Trani shortly after his appointment. Therefore, it came as no surprise when President Trani announced her selection as provost in the fall of 1992.

The manner in which the appointment was handled temporarily strained my relationship with Grace Harris but I soon got over it. Her appointment as the first African American Provost and Vice President of Academic Affairs was significant and in no uncertain terms she earned it and was unquestionably qualified. I understood that, particularly at the executive level, chemistry is as important as credentials and competence. From the onset I was completely devoted to the success of Provost Harris and she acknowledged as much when I left VCU a few years later.

Throughout my career I could never understand why some colleagues were at times uncomfortable when Blacks tend to get along too well. At times when there were two or more successful Black leaders in an organization, invidious comparisons invariably were made. This seemed to be based on a calculus that one Black person had to be smarter than the other, or more trustworthy, or more willing to entertain or tell jokes than the other. Comparisons like these whether intentional or not often contributed to a divide and conquer strategy.

I gave fourteen years of my professional life trying to make VCU live up to its considerable potential. We made lasting friendships on the campus and in the community.

Among the highlights of my return to VCU in 1987 was to be involved in a significant way in the future election of Lawrence Douglas Wilder as governor of the Commonwealth of Virginia. I was at the University of North Carolina Greensboro when then Senator

Wilder was elected lieutenant governor of Virginia. Although I contributed to his campaign, I was not among the many boots on the ground, and I lamented that fact. I missed being an active part of that history and I craved the opportunity to be involved when he ran for Governor. Returning to VCU in 1987 made that possible.

## CHAPTER SEVEN

# Winston-Salem State University

In January 1996, a long time ambition of mine was fulfilled when I was appointed chancellor of Winston-Salem State University by the Board of Governors of the University of North Carolina System. In all candor, although I embraced the opportunity enthusiastically, I really wanted to stay at VCU.

My wife Virginia had returned to work as a school psychologist and was pleased with her new job. Our children were settled in our neighborhood and thriving in school. Why would I want to disrupt everything? I did not, yet it was crystal clear that I had hit a ceiling at VCU and difficult decisions had to be made.

As I look back on my years at VCU and think about former colleagues, the number of Black males who left is striking. Of course, people change jobs for a variety of reasons and I am sure that in some instances these men left VCU for better career opportunities or retirement. Yet, given the paucity of African American males in higher education in the 1990s, one might wonder why so many left and why?

### African American Males at VCU, 1971–1999

L. Victor Collins, 1989–2001
King E. Davis, 1985–1990; 1994–1998; 8/1999–12/1999
Murry N. DePillars, 1971–1995
David M. French, 1992–1996
Dewey Hickman, 1986–1990
Quincy L. Moore, 1985–2001

Alvin J. Schexnider, 1979–1984; 1987–1995
Jackson T. Wright, Jr., 1980–1990

Virginia and I talked about it and weighed our options. I began scanning the *Chronicle of Higher Education* for opportunities at Black colleges across the country. Family was important, so I knew we did not want to move to some far-away place that would limit accessibility to Virginia's parents in Salem. Hence, when the opportunity to go to Winston-Salem State a mere hundred miles away came up, I accepted the challenge. Additionally, Winston-Salem State offered an opportunity for me to build a strong undergraduate liberal arts program that I believed had the potential to distinguish it from other Historically Black Colleges and Universities (HBCUs). I believed then as now that carving a distinctive niche and distinguishing itself from other HBCUs was critical to the future of Winston-Salem State.

The 1980s had ushered in an era of change and innovation in higher education in unexpected ways. Deregulation in the private sector and advancements in information technology brought about a major overhaul in all types of business: airlines, banking, energy, publishing and communications, etc. Higher education was not exempt from all the changes surrounding every conceivable organization. For many institutions, change came slowly and this was true for colleges and universities, especially HBCUs. Confronting this harsh reality was painful, as I was to discover when I arrived at Winston-Salem State in January 1996. That very same semester, Wake Forest University, also in Winston-Salem, announced that each student in its next entering freshman class would receive a laptop computer. This was to be a game-changer that would catapult a selective private university to the forefront of innovation in higher education.

This was the opposite of the situation at Winston-Salem State. Although some technology was in use there, it was uneven and certainly underutilized. My first day on the job, I was surprised to find

**At the author's investiture as Chancellor of Winston-Salem State University with Governor L. Douglas Wilder (left), 1996 (courtesy Winston-Salem State University).**

an IBM Selectric typewriter in use in my office. Winston-Salem State was a part of the University of North Carolina System and therefore required to use state-mandated software and hardware. Yet, somehow the university had been allowed to skirt the rules. I suspect this was because it claimed hardship as an HBCU or perhaps because campus leadership did not insist on meeting system and state requirements. Whatever the explanation, this willful lapse and negligence resulted in frequent audits and irregularities in financial reporting especially.

It was soon clear to me that I had accepted a job that was much more difficult than I had expected and frankly, in some respects, I was ill-prepared to handle. For one, I failed to recognize that Winston-Salem State, like all HBCUs, had a different organizational culture than I was accustomed to at majority schools like Syracuse University, Virginia Commonwealth University and the University of North Carolina Greensboro. This is not to disparage HBCUs because their role and contributions to higher education and society are indisputable. Rather, it is to acknowledge that their unique origins, the challenges they confront, the lack of resources and sometimes the will to meaningfully address them invariably shape the way they operate and conduct business.

My experiences and their implications for my family and career are chronicled in *Saving Black Colleges*, published in 2013, so I will not recount them here. Suffice it to say that what I intended to be a ten-year commitment to repositioning a small Black college turned out to be four years of the most challenging experiences of my entire professional career.

From the onset I expected that my role at Winston-Salem State was that of a change agent. To be perfectly honest, I failed to understand how big a job this would be. In particular, I underestimated the magnitude of the academic, administrative and financial problems there as well as the political obstacles on the campus, within the board of trustees, and within the local community. Being a change agent is fine if the organization is willing to accept a different way of doing things. It did not take long for me to realize that my board and numerous faculty strongly preferred to maintain the status quo. Another major impediment was the president of the Winston-Salem State University Alumni Association who was also an employee of the university. These dual roles created numerous opportunities for conflict since this individual saw himself as a union steward who sought out disgruntled employees like himself to oppose nearly every action aimed at quality improvement.

Eighteen months after I began as chancellor my supervisor, C.D. Spangler, retired as president of the University of North Carolina System. His departure left me without the political support I needed to complete the work I had started. His successor was initially supportive but after a few months she began to distance herself from me claiming that the Black Caucus of the legislature was prepared to issue a vote of no confidence in me. During my last two years as chancellor my administration implemented changes we believed were in the best interests of the university, but without political support from the UNC System and its president, I simply could not withstand the onslaught of negative publicity, and the seemingly continuous drumbeat of criticism of some alumni and locals who resisted the type of change required to render the university competitive.

By June 1998 the system president was headed toward retirement and his successor was soon to follow him that summer. Although the UNC Board of Governors is the governing body for all North Carolina public institutions of higher education, each campus has a board of trustees, which is advisory. True governance resides in the University of North Carolina Board of Governors; however, the existence of a campus-based Board of Trustees leaves considerable room for mischief, often in the form of meddling in the daily operations of the institution. That is exactly what I found when I arrived: board meddling in the administrative affairs of the university.

With President Spangler's help I tried to reduce and eventually eliminate board interference in the daily operation of the university. His successor did not provide a similar level of support. My experience was that Winston-Salem State and other HBCUs in the system were treated differently from UNC and the other majority schools. I suspected as much but hearing it from him was confirmation. The lack of support at the top and growing internal problems made me think about my future at Winston-Salem State University, so I began to explore how I should spend the remainder of my time there.

In fall 1996, not long after my arrival we launched a strategic planning process designed to reposition Winston-Salem State University as a strong, competitive regional institution. Following Spangler's retirement in 1998 when it was apparent that I did not have the support from the top, the implementation of the strategic plan was well underway. We were also preparing for reaffirmation of accreditation by the Commission on Colleges of the Southern Association of

Colleges and Schools (SACS). We coordinated implementation of the strategic plan with reaffirmation of accreditation in order to complete both of these goals and satisfy compliance with Y2K by the end of December 1999.

In early 1999 I was offered the position of vice president for student affairs of the UNC System; I was not interested in that role. My entire background was in academic affairs, and I did not want to accept a job where I could not play to my strengths. Also, this vice presidency was the only one at the System level that a Black person ever held and I refused to be typecast in that role. The system president then began to suggest that I consider a presidency in the California State University System where she had worked previously and had good connections. I had no desire to work in California and I had previously declined an offer of provost at a respected private university there.

After a while, subtle suggestions became unmistakable signs of pressure. I was being thrown to the curb for what I considered I was doing a good job by most objective measures. Winston-Salem State was in dire need of repair and redirection and we were making steady progress, but that did not matter. The system president was feeling pressure so it was applied it to me, vocalizing that time was not on my side or hers. Dr. Thomas Hearn, president of Wake Forest University, was a vocal supporter and recognized the accomplishments underway, at one point, writing a scathing letter regarding the System's failure to protect me from detractors on the board and in the local community. A prominent pastor of the largest Presbyterian Church in town also wrote seeking acknowledgment that the university was moving in the right direction and that the president and the UNC System should show visible support, but again, to no avail.

Consequently, I decided that I would leave after ensuring that the strategic plan was on sound footing and that the university would be adequately prepared for SACS reaffirmation of accreditation and Y2K. I resigned, effective January 6, 2000, after having secured an administrative position at Wake Forest University School of Medicine as director of health policy. Leaving Winston-Salem State University (WSSU) after four years was very difficult, although it was the right decision. It was especially hard since we had made notable progress in several areas. Perhaps most painful was the fact that I was pressured to resign, mainly for political reasons.

Resigning was a bitter pill to swallow also. There is no doubt that I made many mistakes but no one could accuse me of anything illegal, immoral or unethical. The simple truth was that I refused to accept board meddling in the management of the university, I was determined to raise the academic bar eschewing mediocrity and incompetence, and I was not a local homegrown leader, which for some local Black leaders meant that I would never be accepted.

When I announced that I was leaving, the *Winston-Salem Journal*, despite prior portrayals, offered a favorable assessment of my leadership. Previous editorials were sometimes hard-hitting even though my general sense was that we were making giant strides in moving the university forward. I was pleasantly surprised to read what the *Winston-Salem Journal* presented to its readership. On the front page above the fold article, the editor wrote:

> Supporters, opponents praise his vision, work to make the school a leading regional university.... Schexnider, 54, leaves a mixed legacy of strained relations with many university constituencies and undeniable progress in fund-raising and other areas. Molly Broad, the president of the University of North Carolina system, praised him with resolving longstanding accounting problems. "I applaud Chancellor Schexnider's leadership," she said.[1]

In four years, we improved the six-year graduation rate from 39.4 percent to 47.8 percent. In the same period, we doubled the endowment from $9.8 million to $18.8 million. We launched two new master's programs, and replaced academic divisions with professional schools to better reflect degree program offerings and realignments consistent with trends in higher education. However, none of this satisfied the critics. In fact, my major nemesis, whom I had fired for incompetence and who was the ringleader of the campaign to fire me, said in the news article that healing will begin immediately if the next chancellor shares Schexnider's vision, but lacks his sometimes standoffish manner. The chancellor, he said, "had some great ideas, but he was into himself so much."[2] In other words, disdain and dissatisfaction were not as much about my skills, abilities and accomplishments.

Thankfully, I understood this early in my arrival at Winston-Salem State, and it enabled me to decide with confidence that it was best to move on. It became clear that no matter how much we accomplished, I would never satisfy my detractors. In a joint press conference with Wake Forest University President Thomas K. Hearn, I announced my resignation from Winston-Salem State on November 18, 1999. After four very intense years, it was time to move on. I was particularly concerned about the toll that the nearly nonstop criticism and negative media attention had exacted on my family. The university and its alumni leadership had become a circus I concluded, and I wanted no part of it.

Dr. Richard H. Dean, executive vice president for health affairs at Wake Forest University, extended a lifeline that I readily accepted. My new job was director of health policy for the Wake Forest University School of Medicine. In part, this was due to the relationships I established as I sought to create a strategic partnership between Winston-Salem State and Wake Forest in the area of allied health. The leadership at the WFU School of Medicine were enthusiastic about the prospect, but my faculty colleagues at WSSU were not interested. My new job would entail organizing lectures and conferences on various aspects of health policy and, in particular, spotlighting attention on the need for some type of universal health care. Ultimately, this was addressed by the Affordable Care Act, later referred to as Obamacare; but in 2000, when I began my new job, this was a dream rather than reality.

I was at once grateful for the opportunity to start a new job, but also pained by the circumstances under which I left Winston-Salem State. Leading a Black college had been an ambition that I courted assiduously. As well, I had worked hard to achieve a measure of success under very difficult circumstances. Yet, here I was leaving an organization on whose behalf I, my family, and colleagues had worked so hard, to someone else, mainly because of politics, petty jealousies, and a resistance to change. I deliberately waited until the end of the fall 1999 semester to announce my resignation.

As the *Winston-Salem Journal* noted, the departure came "after perhaps the quietest months of his tenure...." "I always intended to exit on a high note and that's precisely what I'm doing," Schexnider said. "The university is in very good condition."[3] The simple truth is that I was physically exhausted and emotionally drained. From July 1998, when the president who hired me left, until I announced my resignation at the end of 1999, I felt as though I had been under constant attack. I looked tired and distraught, because I was. Our family needed a break from the constant harangue of the media, but we also needed to get away for a well-deserved respite.

We decided that a family vacation was a priority. Even though we knew that we would need to leave the chancellor's residence and find a home to move into, we felt it was more important to go to a place where we could relax and recharge our batteries. We spent the Christmas holidays at Atlantis in the Bahamas, a place where adults and children could find enjoyment. Finding a place to live would have to wait until we returned. When we returned from the Bahamas, we were fortunate to find a house to rent not far from the chancellor's residence, and not far from our children's schools. I took the entire month of January 2000 off. I began my new position at Wake Forest on February 1. I was fortunate to bring my administrative assistant, Teresa Harnish, with me. Teresa had been my assistant since 1987 at VCU, and later followed me to Winston-Salem State. Several months before I announced I was leaving, I helped Teresa find work at Womble Carlyle, a leading law firm in Winston-Salem. I was pleased when she later agreed to join me at Wake Forest University School of Medicine.

## CHAPTER EIGHT

# Norfolk State University, 2002–2007

My appointment at Wake Forest University was never intended to be permanent. Frankly, I was uncertain about what to do next. I was clear about not pursuing just any presidency, especially a presidency of an HBCU. I felt I had been burned by my own people, which made it doubly painful because my intentions were always about serving others. I came to do good, but what did it profit me? There was also the reality that my tenure at Winston-Salem State had generated considerable hostility and negative media attention, so much that I was viewed with suspicion or doubt about my competence and ability. This was most painful. I had blown all that I had worked so hard for in terms of my professional reputation. Now, I had to start building all over again.

Our son was in high school so we decided he should graduate in Winston-Salem rather than being uprooted. Our daughter was two years behind him and, in her freshman year, joined him at Mount Tabor High School. While we were happy they attended the same high school near our home, this was an especially difficult experience for our daughter, and I bear a considerable amount of guilt for putting her in an environment she was not prepared to handle. Academically, she excelled, but the rough and tumble social climate of a public high school were totally different from what she had been accustomed to in a sedate Catholic school milieu.

After almost two and a half years at Wake Forest University, in July 2002 I had an opportunity to go to Norfolk State University (NSU) as interim executive vice president. At the urging of the Board of Visitors, Dr. Marie V. McDemmond, president, hired me to manage the day-to-day operations of the university. All of the vice presidents reported to me which enabled President McDemmond to focus more attention on external relations and fundraising. Patrick B. Kelly, a former VCU colleague, had accepted the position of general counsel of Norfolk State University. Pat and I had stayed in touch and when he learned that I was exploring job opportunities he brought me to the attention of Dr. McDemmond. I began my tenure at Norfolk State on an interim basis, and in January 2003 the job was made permanent, and I signed a five-year contract.

In June 2004, President McDemmond went on a six-month sabbatical and I became Acting President. She returned in January 2005 looking wan and tired. The following month she disclosed to me that she had been diagnosed with lymphoma and was retiring to devote attention to her health. Although I resumed my permanent position as executive vice president, in point of fact, because President McDemmond was gone most of the time attending to her health I continued to lead the university. When she officially retired in June 2005, I was appointed interim president for the 2005–2006 academic year. In effect, I led the university from June 2004 until July 2006, when a new president was installed. I was happy to step in when the university really needed me, but I was transparent about not wanting the job permanently.

Actually, it had been a mild challenge reassuring Marie McDemmond that I was there to help her succeed rather than feathering my own nest. I learned many things at NSU, including the fact that a former president is often viewed with suspicion, if not by the boss, but those around her. I once told her that I sensed that people around her were spreading rumors about my lack of loyalty; she acknowledged the hearsay but that did not stop the mistrust. After Winston-Salem State, I had already decided I would not seek another presidency.

I started a one-year appointment as interim president of Norfolk State University on July 1, 2005. With more than twenty years of executive level experience, I had a feel for the university, its challenges and its opportunities. I also had a good working relationship with the university's senior leadership, middle managers (deans and department chairs), faculty and staff. Most importantly, I enjoyed a good working relationship with the Norfolk State University Board of Visitors. The Board's Rector, Jack L. Ezzell, Jr., was an exceptional leader who understood the role of a governing board.

Unlike the Board of Trustees at Winston-Salem State, the NSU Board of Visitors generally did not seek to insert itself in the daily operations of the university. If a board member tried to interfere, Rector Ezzell was adept at handling the situation. Jack Ezzell understood the importance of a good working relationship between the president and the board chair. These two individuals have the greatest influence on board effectiveness. A highly successful businessman, Mr. Ezzell was a savvy executive, a man of great integrity, and he was widely respected in the region and across the state. I was especially grateful that unlike some board chairs he had no desire to be the power behind the throne.

It was also important that I continue to build relationships with key external stakeholders—alumni, business and civic leaders, and City Hall. I understood that the nature of the job had changed noticeably in recent years. Whereas, in former times, the job of a college president was that of an academic leader, today, a college or university president spends half or more of his or her time in external activities, particularly fund-raising. This meant that the internal operations of the university had to be solid and reliable. For Black colleges and universities, where administrative operations sometimes underperformed, greater attention was required in order to ensure smooth functioning of the institution. Although my position was interim and I had no desire to seek it permanently, I dedicated my efforts to moving the university forward in every possible way. Listed below are key accomplishments during my one-year interim presidency.

---

## Key Accomplishments July 2005 to June 2006

- Secured the largest gift in the history of the university, one million dollars, from an alumnus.
- Oversaw the planning, design and construction of the RISE Center, later renamed the McDemmond Center for Applied Research.
- Chaired and supervised the development and implementation of the Norfolk State University Strategic Plan 2004–2009. Among its major achievements are improvements in campus design and construction and renovation of facilities, including building the first new academic building in two decades.
- Established a working relationship between NSU, City of Norfolk, and the Norfolk Redevelopment and Housing Authority (NRHA) to ensure NSU received equal treatment with Old Dominion University in the development of the City's master Plan.
- Secured title to the old Norfolk Community Hospital in order to expand the university's footprint to accommodate new construction. Acquisition of this land enabled the university to construct its first co-educational student residence, a new public safety building, a new student commons, and the construction of another co-educational dormitory.
- Secured funding for construction of a new Lyman Beecher Brooks Library.
- Established an Enrollment Management Office and recruited, trained and mentored its first leader in order that NSU could compete more effectively for students in the region.
- Led and provided oversight of an economic impact study to document the university's role in contributing to the economic vitality of the City of Norfolk and the Hampton Roads region.

- Commissioned a comprehensive review of campus police operations resulting in a major overhaul of university safety and security and improved police cooperation under a new inter-jurisdictional agreement with area law enforcement agencies.
- Oversaw creation of the university's own information technology department, a mission-critical function that had been previously outsourced with major risk to the university's entire computer network. I also recruited and mentored the director of this new department.

A president of Norfolk State University was appointed following a national search. Dr. Carolyn Meyers began her new job on July 1, 2006. I returned to my position as executive vice president under the terms of a contract through December 31, 2007. The Board of Visitors encouraged me to help the new president with the transition and, of course, I was happy to do so. When it became apparent that the new administration was confident in its ability to lead I began contemplating an exit strategy and plans for retirement. Also, the timing was right since our son had graduated from college and our daughter was in her second year of college.

One of the challenges of presidential transitions is that a new leader may be tempted to scrub or dismantle a predecessor's accomplishments to assert themselves and fortify the role. Sometimes circumstances require decisive action but this should not be whimsical or personal. It is critically important that governing boards exercise their fiduciary responsibilities to the institution so that successful initiatives and plans are not scuttled simply because a new leader is in place. In too many instances presidential transitions become mired in who is on what team—the outgoing administration or the incoming one? Dissatisfaction with the outgoing administration and fear of the new president's agenda, abetted by distrust and academic politics, can be destabilizing and harmful to the institution. I preferred to stay at least through December 2007 but that's not the way things turned out.

Under the leadership of President McDemmond Norfolk State had begun to carve out a niche in applied research. President McDemmond sought to establish NSU as a STEM (science, technology, engineering and math) powerhouse. She articulated this vision well and faculty and staff promoted it in their teaching and research. McDemmond provided the concept for a new building that would serve as the nerve center for this new space that NSU had begun to carve for itself. This was smart because HBCUs must be able to distinguish themselves from the competition.

**Alvin and Elena at Morehouse College, 2001 (author's collection).**

The board's selection of the new president was intentional. On paper, it appeared that the new leader had all the right qualifications to build on her predecessor's vision and, in the words of several board members, to "take Norfolk State to the next level."

When I went to Winston-Salem State in 1996, my goal was to stay ten years, write a book and consult. Although I did not meet my objective, I was able to serve as chancellor four years, for which I am grateful. I did not want another presidency and Norfolk State was never on my radar; however, a major enticement was the

The author (left) with Governor Tim Kaine (right) and Rector Jack L. Ezzell, Jr., at Norfolk State University, 2006 (courtesy Norfolk State University).

opportunity to return to Virginia, so that my wife's parents, now in their eighties, could move to be near us. This meant a lot to all of us and it brought the family in closer contact. Thus, when the Norfolk State opportunity surfaced, we were pleased to accept it.

About a year before leaving Norfolk State, I started a consulting practice and developed a relationship with the Association of Governing Boards of Universities and Colleges (AGB). I also continued to work on the book, which frankly entailed several revisions to cool the passion and anger resulting from my experiences at Winston-Salem State. I was determined that the book would be helpful and informative on both the general and unique requirements related to leadership at HBCUs, namely, change management, strategic planning and particularly, board governance. I did not want the book to be an angry screed or a diatribe against all Black colleges and universities. That would be patently wrong and unfair. Equally important, it would have served no useful purpose. To denigrate all Black colleges and universities based on my singular experience could never be justified. Certainly, some facets were generalizable, but not all.

My goal was to be helpful by sharing insights gained from direct personal experience, tempered by pragmatism and objectivity. When *Saving Black Colleges* was finally published in 2013, I felt a sense of relief that it was now in print, but also some measure of satisfaction that in writing a book that gave an insider's perspective on what it is like to lead a Black college and to be a change agent, I had honored the physician's credo: "First, do no harm." Despite their unassailable contributions, Black colleges and universities remain undervalued. The last thing I would ever want to do is denigrate or put them down.

My consulting practice increased following retirement and I was adjusting nicely to my new lifestyle that included more reading, travel, and attending classic car shows. Eighteen months later, I received a call that would alter my plans and interrupt retirement.

## CHAPTER NINE

# Thomas Nelson Community College, 2008–2011

In the summer of 2008 I received a call from Dr. Glenn Dubois, chancellor of the Virginia Community College System (VCCS) in Richmond. I had never met Dr. Dubois or worked at a community college. Later, I learned that he called me on the recommendation of Dr. Deborah DiCroce, president of Tidewater Community College (TCC), one of the largest in the system with campuses in Norfolk, Virginia Beach, Chesapeake, and Portsmouth. Chancellor Dubois was calling to see if I would be interested in a one-year appointment as acting president of Thomas Nelson Community College in Hampton, Virginia, about 32 miles from our home in Chesapeake.

Dr. Dubois was tentative in our discussions about the need for a change in leadership at TNCC. Frankly, I had no knowledge of the circumstances surrounding an impending transition and neither did I know anything about the college. The president was Dr. Charles Taylor, an African American whom I had not met. In addition, I had never set foot on the campus. My only experience with a community college was at J. Sergeant Reynolds Community College in Richmond related to my work at VCU.

To its credit, in the 1980s VCU had begun meaningful efforts toward developing an articulation agreement with J. Sargeant Reynolds whereby students could transfer credits toward a degree at VCU. This required laborious time-consuming review of courses by faculty of both institutions to ensure that selected community college courses met the expectations of VCU faculty. This was prudent because increasingly J. Sargeant Reynolds became a major source of enrollment for VCU and that relationship evolved as a model for implementation across the entire Virginia Community College System. In time, one institution in particular, Tidewater Community College (TCC), established a slogan that proved to be highly effective: "From here go anywhere." In fact, TCC was so successful that it began to siphon enrollments from Norfolk State University, whose decline in students had continued for several years.

As Chancellor Dubois and I continued to talk about the possibility of my coming to Thomas Nelson Community College, it was clear that the problems engulfing President Taylor were closely related to race. Although I understand that race is difficult to talk about, my approach is to be direct about everything and so I put this on the table. Dubois reluctantly acknowledged that yes, race was an issue that had spilled over into the local community with potentially exacerbating race relations consequences in the region.

Blatantly racist blogs and posts on social media were widespread with little to nothing being done to counter it. I recognized that accepting the job might appear to some that I was being used to displace another Black man. At the same time, I accepted the fact that this was an opportunity not only to correct a problem but also to set the college on a better path with improved race relations and a restored sense of civility and collegiality among all stakeholders, but particularly, African American students, faculty, staff, and alumni.

The incumbent president was a good leader who through no fault of his own encountered difficult challenges, many of which were related to race. His predecessor was an African American woman president who probably encountered some of the same problems but perhaps was better adept at managing them. If I have learned anything about race relations in my personal life and professional career, it is that White males often feel more comfortable dealing with African American women than with African American men. This has been my experience totally and without exception. It took a while for officials to acknowledge that racism was a factor in the president's departure from the college so I had to decide whether I wanted to accept this appointment knowing that I had likely been selected to ease the impact of the exit of a Black man.

Accepting a job in the aftermath of the dismissal of an African American was not a position I wanted to be in, ever. My wife and I had several conversations about whether I should accept the offer. I also discussed it with my close friend and confidant, Jack L. Ezzell, Jr., former rector of the Board of Visitors at Norfolk State. Jack had a successful career as an Air Force intelligence officer before retiring as a colonel. He earned an MBA from Ohio State University and started a highly successful global information security company, ZelTech LLC. I trusted Jack's advice completely and I knew he would be candid and forthright. Jack believed I could be helpful and that I could turn things around, so with his and my wife's encouragement, I agreed to accept the position.

I began a one-year appointment as interim president of Thomas Nelson Community College on October 1, 2008. When I arrived, faculty and administration relations required immediate attention. The discord was openly racial and constantly exacerbated by blogs on social media and in the local newspaper. For example, the vice president for academic affairs and a dean, both White, openly opposed the creation of a dental hygiene program that had been approved by the College and the Virginia Community College System and endorsed by the local dental association. A highly qualified finalist for the position of program director was not given serious consideration despite presenting impeccable credentials.

Within my first year I re-opened the search process for a program director. The finalist who was treated unfairly previously applied again, was recommended by the search committee and was subsequently hired. He built a very strong dental hygiene program whose graduates consistently had a 100 percent pass rate on the dental hygiene examination.

My work was cut out for me. The first order of business was to repair relations between the administration and the faculty and to signal that I was serious about making needed changes. Early on,

I convened a meeting of the entire campus and invited the system chancellor, Dr. Glenn DuBois, to attend. I asked him to offer remarks and to lend his support, which he did.

Within a few months of my arrival, I appointed a blue ribbon commission composed of faculty, staff, students, and key campus stakeholders to address the issues and present recommendations. Its composition was intentional and included ringleaders of the opposition, a couple of deans and department chairs along with faculty senate kingpins. When our work was finished we achieved consensus on a code of ethical and professional conduct that was printed and displayed in offices and classrooms throughout campus. I believed it was important to involve key leaders and stakeholders in developing a compact that would establish rules of civility and ethical conduct. We might not be able to change attitudes, but I was convinced we could alter behavior. It did not take long for us to witness some measure of success.

Gradually, things began to improve. The sniping and open hostilities became less frequent and social media comments toned down somewhat. Sometimes when efforts are made to restore or repair, more time and attention are required than originally planned. This was my experience at TNCC. What began as a one-year assignment morphed into a three-year commitment. That is because, once I had an opportunity to examine the institution closely, I could not leave until additional corrections were made. The college had been experiencing problems in several areas in academic affairs, student affairs and campus climate, much of it related to race.

During my interim appointment I found several major issues that I felt required immediate attention. Rather than leave them to my successor, I felt that as a leader I had a responsibility to tackle some rather thorny issues head-on instead of kicking the can down the road, so to speak. Mainly, these were glaring problems in student affairs, academic affairs, information technology, and fundraising. We made notable progress in clearing the deck for the next president, and I felt good about leaving TNCC in much better shape than I found it.

When I announced plans to leave in spring 2011, an editorial in the *Daily Progress*, the local newspaper, had this to say:

Alvin Schexnider came in as president during a tumultuous time at Thomas Nelson Community College, and righted a careening ship. The school's faculty was in pretty much open revolt against the former president when Schexnider came in as interim president in mid–2008, and later signed on for another two years. Schexnider immediately established a new tone at the helm of TNCC. With 30 years of experience in higher education, Schexnider began a new code of ethics and focused on making expectations clearer. He also began a diversity institute for faculty and staff, reorganized student affairs, focused on customer service, and started a Presidential Leadership Institute. Though his departure was planned, we are sorry to see Schexnider stepping aside.[1]

# CHAPTER TEN

# Race and the Academy

The eminent scholar W.E.B. Dubois famously remarked that "the problem of the twentieth century is the color line." There is no gainsaying the fact that considerable progress has occurred since those prophetic words were first uttered. The simple truth is that twenty-three years into the twenty-first century, in the vernacular of the moment, "race still matters." Dr. Dubois spent his entire professional life as an academician and civil rights leader, yet, disgusted and disillusioned by racism in American society, he exiled himself to Ghana, West Africa, where he died in 1963, within days of Dr. Martin Luther King's leading the largest march for civil rights in the nation's history.

Dr. Dubois was a co-founder of the National Association for the Advancement of Colored People (NAACP) that laid the groundwork for Blacks' achieving equality and first-class citizenship. His outstanding research and writings and his activism paved the way for the March on Washington, yet he was not there to witness or participate in this historic event. Instead, he died in the distant land of our forebears, indeed, in itself a noteworthy statement.

In his final book, *Mirror to America*, the eminent historian John Hope Franklin reflected on the persistence of race and its effect on every facet of society including the academy. Of course, that was a shared experience of countless others and it continues to this day. Speaking of society, Franklin observed: "Born in 1915, I grew up in a racial climate that was stifling to my senses and demeaning to my emotional health and well-being."[1]

He then recounts several incidents whereby he was victimized by racism from age six to eighty including being removed from a train, nearly lynched, and asked to "hang a white guest's coat where he was not an employee but a member."[2] Life in the academy for a Black man or woman was slightly sweeter, but hardly utopian. By the mid–1950s, barely in his forties, John Hope Franklin had established a solid reputation as one of the nation's leading historians—Black or White. He had authored three books, including the seminal and still widely used *From Slavery to Freedom*, yet the leading universities paid him no mind. That changed, however, when Brooklyn College extended an offer to Franklin to join its faculty. He wrote:

> In 1956, it was almost inconceivable that a group of white scholars at a predominantly white institution would seriously entertain the possibility of having me join them as their colleague and their chairman. My brief teaching stints at Harvard, Wisconsin, and Cornell were fresh in my mind, and I was quite certain that most historians at those institutions never gave a second thought to my affiliation with them except on a most temporary basis. Brooklyn College's overture was of a different order entirely. Their invitation was that I join the faculty, not for a summer or a semester, but permanently![3]

John Hope Franklin's faculty appointment at Brooklyn College was so unusual that it made the front page of *The New York Times*. That was then, but this is now. Contrast Franklin's appointment in 1956 with today and it becomes crystal clear how little progress has been made seven decades later. In a *Chronicle of Higher Education* essay cleverly entitled "Becoming Full Professor While Black," Marlene Daut, an African American woman on the faculty of one of the leading institutions of higher education in the country, offered this wry assessment of a signal achievement in her career:

> My promotion last month brings the number of black female full professors in the College of Arts and Sciences at the University of Virginia, where I am now appointed, to a paltry three. Across the United States, black women are only about 2 percent of all full professors. That is at least better than the situation in Britain, where the number of black female professors at any rank stands at a total of 25, but it is still rather dismal given that black people make up 13 percent of the U.S. population.[4]

Obviously, a lot has changed since my first faculty appointment in 1973 at Southern University in Baton Rouge, Louisiana, as an assistant professor of political science. The decision to work at an HBCU was intentional; however, to my faculty advisors, this was unthinkable. In many respects this was understandable since HBCUs were totally foreign to many Whites who did not know they existed and, if they did know, questioned or disparaged them. More than 100 Black colleges had been established since Reconstruction yet, like Ralph Ellison's *Invisible Man*, many were unseen and ignored. When they were recognized often it was in the most demeaning and disrespectful ways. In a lengthy *Harvard Educational Review* article two respected academics, Christopher Jencks and David Riesman, published the following critique without any empirical data to support their damning assertions:

> ...Negro colleges today face many of the same dilemmas as these white institutions.... Such colleges will educate mostly Negroes who will work behind the wall of segregation. Although these institutions are likely to survive, and indeed to educate a substantial proportion of all Negro undergraduates, they are also likely to remain academically inferior institutions.[5]

When contrasting private and public HBCUs the authors are even more strident in their assertions:

> Like the poorer private Negro colleges, then, public Negro colleges are for the most part likely to remain fourth-rate institutions at the tail end of the academic procession.[6]

Such was the belief system and prevailing perceptions and attitude when I began my academic career in September 1973. My mentor, Dr. David Minar, chairman of political science at Northwestern University, expressed a fervent wish that I would join the faculty of a Big Ten university where I could serve as a role model. I respected Dr. Minar a lot and entertained the idea, but not seriously.

Although I had been selected the top first year graduate student by the political science faculty, it had been very challenging. I overcame lack of preparation with sheer grit and determination. I discovered in high school that some of my classmates were probably smarter, but no one worked harder than me. I came to Northwestern directly from Vietnam and I was determined to succeed at all costs. Crucial to achieving success was treating life as a graduate student the same way I handled a regular job. I took every course seriously. I devoted several hours for study each day, and if I needed help in a particular subject, I was not shy about seeking tutoring. Never strong in math, I had difficulty with statistics, and sought and received help from a fellow classmate.

While I was being encouraged to be a role model at a Big Ten School, the department of political science was struggling to build rapport with its own role model, "Michael Johnson," a tenured associate professor of political science who was its lone Black member. The first year curriculum was highly structured and did not allow for many options. I did not take one of "Professor Johnson's" courses, but I found him to be a valuable mentor and advisor. At the end of my first year of graduate study, I seriously considered dropping out of the program. Thankfully, he talked me out of it.

At Northwestern, graduate students were regarded as junior faculty. We were on a first-name basis with faculty and occasionally consulted on department issues. Dr. "Michael Johnson" was Mike to us; I could talk to him openly, and on some matters, he confided in me. I noticed that he did not spend much time in the department. He seemed distant from his faculty colleagues. He was its lone Black member, and in retrospect, that must have been a heavy burden. Years later, when I found myself in a similar situation as the lone Black on the faculty or in an administrative position, I was able to comprehend what Mike was experiencing. On a couple of occasions Mike's colleagues made comments about his lack of involvement in department activities. I mentioned this to him once, not realizing that I was probably being used. Mike's advice was that our conversations must be strictly confidential and not to be shared with anyone.

I then understood the chasm but also the boundaries. The last thing Mike or I needed was for me to be used as a conduit for anyone seeking information about a colleague. The department had one Black member who was exceptional in so many ways, yet was treated as an outsider. This was the early 1970s; at the time, Northwestern had only a handful of Black faculty. If a department had any, it was likely to be one: in history, Sterling Stuckey; in economics, Marcus Alexis; in sociology, Jim Pitts; in law, Thomas Todd; and in education, Dolores Cross. These were all not so subtle reminders of the role of race in the recruitment and hiring of Blacks in the academy. It was also indicative of the lack of availability of Black faculty.

In fall 1972, several first-year Black students in the department of political science decided to confront the lack of Black faculty head-on. We felt strongly that the department should aggressively recruit Black faculty. I was tasked with the job of preparing a statement, the Black Graduate Students Manifesto, demanding the hiring of additional Black faculty. Here is an excerpt from that manifesto:

> It seems that the prevailing attitude among some faculty members is to resign themselves to the reality that having black graduate students is an expedient to be accepted for the present. In the interim we will be run through the mill in expiation of past department sins.[7]

Several conversations both formal and informal followed. The refrain "we can't find any qualified Blacks to hire" invariably surfaced every time the issue was raised. We were undeterred. Ultimately, the department agreed to recruit another Black political scientist. Although we were not certain, we suspected that Mike was unhappy and contemplating leaving. It's also likely that the department had a similar intuition and viewed our importuning as a wise move in anticipation of Mike's possible departure.

Despite the fact that the faculty was convinced that none could be found, three Black political scientists, all men, were brought in for interview: Wilbur Rich from Wayne State University, Frank Morris from MIT, and Michael Preston from the University of California,

Berkeley. Rich had completed his doctorate; Morris and Preston were close to finishing theirs.

Following campus interviews an offer was extended to "John Smith." Because he held an MPA and had extensive work experience with a federal agency Smith desired to enter at the rank of associate professor and at a salary commensurate with his government pay. For a department that had to be pushed into hiring a second Black person, these expectations were not warmly received. An offer was eventually extended and Smith was hired as an associate professor of political science. I subsequently completed my degree and left at the end of the year. I don't know how long Smith remained at Northwestern. I do know that this was a fraught period in higher education as countless Black Ph.D.'s who were recruited to White universities and colleges across the country failed to secure tenure.[8]

## *The Continuing Significance of Race*

American universities and colleges are generally perceived as progressive, even liberal institutions. After all, some of the most strident social protests involving students and faculty have sprouted on university and college campuses (e.g., University of California, Berkeley; Columbia; Harvard; Kent State; etc.). Yet, so-called objective research on race, eugenics and intelligence has produced and promoted racist theories at some of the most vaunted institutions of higher learning. The role of colleges and universities contributing to conservative and reactionary public policies is well-documented. Suffice it to say, the academy is not immune to racism.

During an academic career that spanned more than four decades it goes without saying that I witnessed and experienced subtle but usually overt racism. Whether an act or comment was intentional, the outcome was the same. I fought racial prejudice and anyone who showed signs of it. It took a while, but eventually I learned that you don't have to win every battle to win the war. I learned to choose my battles carefully knowing that how I handled a particular situation could affect my career. Also, countless times there were blatant, clear actions or comments that I viewed as racist. When they occurred, I did not hesitate to call someone out.

There was a price to be paid and each time I had to weigh the cost of speaking. I also discovered that after a while, because I was seen as the guy who always confronted racial issues, some of my colleagues became dismissive of me. It took a while but eventually I learned that having an ally, even a reluctant one to carry water could be helpful to the cause, a stratagem I learned to employ. In far too many instances, it was a lonely journey, but I sallied forth anyway.

What I also found interesting throughout my career is that the system seemed capable of having only one African American in a top leadership position, and if they could get away with it, that one person would be a woman because such an appointment would count for two: Black and female.

## Affirmative Action and Equal Employment Opportunity (AA/EEO)

When I began my academic career in 1973, affirmative action and equal employment opportunity (AA/EEO) programs in higher education were in the early stages of development. In general, the academy took a cautious approach, stressing moderation and obsessing over ensuring that Blacks absolutely must be qualified. The persons hired to lead and oversee affirmative action and equal employment opportunity offices usually found themselves in nearly impossible situations. Some AA/EEO officers were mere window-dressing; they knew it and the schools that hired them knew it. Some were genuinely committed to the recruitment and hiring of Black faculty and staff. The individuals hired to lead these efforts had the difficult task of confronting decades of institutional racism and an organizational culture that resisted change. A Black professor interested in applying for a job at a White university or college had to determine if a particular opportunity was real and whether investment of his or her time and energy was worth the effort.

The AA/EEO officers hired for these positions were sometimes ill-equipped to handle the job. In some instances faculty members who failed to achieve tenure were hired as an affirmative action officer, even though they had no experience in the field. Not once did I ever consider working in affirmative action. I always viewed myself as a faculty member committed to meeting the demands of my profession. That may have been lost on my faculty colleagues but not on me. I felt that once I had established myself as a solid member of the academy, I would be in a better position to take on broader responsibilities as an academic administrator and thereby effect change. As an academic leader I believed I would be able to provide oversight and ensure that policies and procedures existed to foster equality of opportunity without regard for race or gender. My goal was to help shape the organizational culture in ways that would persist long after I was gone. I was convinced that leadership was essentially about making a difference in people's lives. I knew that leadership entails risks and requires courage and that not every leader views the role this way, but those were my terms, and I did not waiver.

Individuals seek leadership positions for various reasons. Some see leadership as an opportunity to wield power. Others like the attention it brings, the pomp and circumstance. In far too many instances we have leaders who want the title, but not the job. They are not at all interested in tackling thorny issues or doing the heavy lifting that is required to achieve significant outcomes. I call such "leaders" benchwarmers or lapdogs because they have no real intention of taking any action that will upset the status quo. Having reached what many may perceive as the pinnacle of success, they are, in the words of my friend and former colleague, Jackson T. Wright, Jr., "so happy to be here." This is not a trite observation. Let me expand on it.

## So Happy to Be Here

At nearly every majority institution where I have worked I got the distinct impression from several White colleagues that I should be "so happy to be here." That is to say, despite or maybe because of my qualifications, I should be demonstrably grateful for having been hired or promoted, as though I did not earn or deserve to hold a position or title. The degree of this attitude may have varied from one university to another, but the sentiment was omnipresent, palpable and unmistakable. Clifton Wharton, Jr., who achieved many "firsts" in an extraordinary career marked by distinction in a broad array of pursuits, described it this way:

> In later life, I found that even a strong record of accomplishment was not enough; when you moved to a new situation, you had to deal with the negative expectations syndrome all over again and start from scratch to eliminate it.... Of course this experience is not unique to me. High-achieving Blacks confront it regularly throughout the United States.[9]

Even for the most accomplished Black man or woman, the expectation is that you must prove yourself worthy to be among Whites never ends. Whether as the lone Black faculty member in a department or one of a handful of other Blacks pursuing an academic administrative career and irrespective of the number, discipline or professional field, African Americans are always under scrutiny and expected to prove themselves in ways that their White colleagues are not.

The admissions scandals a few years ago involving several elite universities across the country brought fresh attention to the influence of wealth in college admissions, its implications for the admission of less privileged African Americans and racial discrimination in general in higher education. For several weeks, stories about the scandals dominated the media. In response, the *Chronicle of Higher Education* published several articles written by graduate students, junior professors and senior scholars about "what it's like to be an African-American academic today." This is the way one Black academic, Stefan Bradley, summed it up:

> I have studied or worked at six predominantly white universities. I have observed the way black professionals survive. Their careers are mostly safe if they express gratitude (whether sincere or not) to the institution; generally go along with whatever their white colleagues want; out produce their peers but do not conspicuously outshine them; if male, avoid suspicions of impropriety with female students (particularly nonblack students); never raise their voice or make sudden moves except at a university sporting event; do not question the institution's sincerity with regard to "diversity" without first reassuring the "allies" that they are doing their very best; and never—ever—forget to smile.[10]

Advocating for diversity, despite its noble, principled call, also carries major risks and potential pitfalls. Michael Fortner spoke of his experience:

> I've witnessed otherwise open-minded white colleagues take umbrage at sincere calls for equity, viewing such requests as personal indictments. I've also seen faculty members of color dismissed or disparaged for agitating for diversity. I've seen them get labeled as "difficult" and "uncooperative" for recognizing their own value and guarding their interests and voice. For minority faculty members, "good" citizenship often means adhering to norms and procedures that can limit diversity and freedom of thought.[11]

I spent almost fourteen years as a faculty member and academic administrator at Virginia Commonwealth University (VCU). The Black Education Association (BEA) was our vehicle to provide mutual support, and to lean on the administration of which I was a part to address concerns related to increasing our numbers and achieving our professional goals.

Always at the top of our list was securing support to increase the number of Black faculty and staff. We found genuine support in Provost Charles Ruch. In 1990 he provided funds to host a two-day retreat of Black faculty and staff at the Moton Center in Gloucester, Virginia, where we discussed strategies regarding faculty recruitment and retention along with an action plan to address them. One highly successful outcome of the retreat was the creation of a mentorship program that paired senior Black faculty with recently hired Black faculty to help prepare for promotion and tenure as well as an orientation about how to navigate racial issues within a large, complex university with two campuses, and two distinctively different organizational cultures.

At the time VCU was still grappling with what it meant to be a university with essentially two distinct organizations—an academic campus that aspired to be a traditional university and the MCV campus, formerly a stand-alone medical college with allied health schools that viewed its sister campus across town with doubt, if not disdain. Within this environment, VCU's academic campus though far from ideal, tended to be more accepting of hiring and promoting Blacks than the MCV campus. To underscore this point, it was not until the late 1980s that a Black faculty member was awarded tenure at the MCV Campus. Jackson T. Wright, Jr., M.D., Ph.D., was promoted to associate professor with tenure in the Department of Medicine. A few years later, Dr. Wright was recruited by Case Western Reserve University School of Medicine, where he enjoyed a highly successful career and earned an international reputation as a leading scientist and clinical professor.

Dr. Wright was also instrumental in another very important aspect of our professional and personal lives. He was the founder and convenor of "the clinic," a weekly Friday afternoon gathering of Black male faculty and staff at a watering hole on the south side of Richmond. Although to outsiders it presented a purely social gathering, in point of fact, "the clinic" was an invaluable source of information sharing, mutual support and cathartic relief from the racism we experienced in our respective jobs.

The BEA was instrumental in the recruitment, hiring and retention of Black faculty and staff, but also in helping the university in other ways that VCU did not fully recognize or appreciate. For example, VCU was slow to understand that its Black alumni, faculty, and staff were a major untapped resource and asset. In the early 1990s I worked closely with Murry DePillars, dean of the School of the Arts, and Grace Harris, social work dean and later VCU's first African American provost, to create the VCU Black Alumni Council. We recognized the need to reach out to many Black alumni who were disengaged from VCU including some who had graduated feeling less than positive about their experiences there. We believed we should reach out and reclaim Black alumni because it was the right thing to do, but also because they were a source of potential support to the university's long-term advancement interests. Through BEA, Black faculty and staff played a major role in launching the Black Alumni Council and pursuing broader university goals.

Equally important to VCU's success were the personal and professional relationships the university's Black faculty and staff enjoyed with Richmond's Black leadership class. Unequivocally, these connections were beneficial to VCU. Often, these relationships were taken for granted, even though they made a material and substantive difference in securing favorable political and legislative outcomes as VCU sought to expand its footprint in the city.

In addition to BEA, a small core of Blacks led by faculty and administrators at Virginia Tech founded a group called the Virginia Association of Black Faculty and Staff to promote the involvement and professional development of Blacks in Virginia higher education. Dr. Joyce Williams-Green, assistant provost at Virginia Tech, spearheaded the organization and provided excellent leadership. Dr. Williams-Green soon enlisted support from faculty and staff at the University of Virginia, James Madison University, Virginia Commonwealth University and Washington and Lee University, the lone private school in the organization. The mission of the group was similar to BEA's except that it was a statewide initiative.

The group received little to no support from the universities where its members were employed, with the exception of Virginia

Tech, where Dr. Williams-Green was assistant provost. Also, President Harrison Wilson hosted a reception at his home when the group met on his campus of Norfolk State University. Mainly, Black faculty and staff were taken for granted, underutilized and undervalued, despite their contributions to the success of public higher education in Virginia.

## Improving Faculty Diversity in Higher Education

During the past five decades, American colleges and universities have experienced major demographic shifts in their makeup regarding race, ethnicity, gender, and international student representation. This is especially true for a dramatic increase in the number of African American students enrolled in White colleges and universities. For most of the twentieth century, for example, the vast majority of Black students attended Black colleges and universities. In fact, these schools, commonly referred to as HBCUs (Historically Black Colleges and Universities), enjoyed a pure monopoly on Black students and faculty.

The 1954 Supreme Court decision *Brown v. Board of Education of Topeka* ushered in a new era that led to the desegregation of secondary and post-secondary education. Consequently, today, nine out of ten African American students attend a White college or university. The hiring of African American faculty has not increased at the same rate as the enrollment of African American students, however. A recent report from the American Council on Education, revealed that 75 percent of faculty at American colleges and universities are White. Conversely, only 6 percent are faculty of color (African American and other racial and ethnic groups), while African American student enrollment stands at 14 percent. Latinx faculty comprise 5 percent, while Latinx student enrollment comprises 14 percent.[12]

A study of faculty diversity at 40 selective public universities by Diyi Li and Cory Koedel discovered even greater disparities. In a comparison of STEM (Science, Technology, Engineering and Mathematics) fields with non–STEM areas (biology, chemistry, economics, educational leadership and policy), Li and Koedel found that "Black, Hispanic, and female faculty are underrepresented relative to their U.S. population shares, whereas Asian, White and male faculty are overrepresented. Overall, Black, Hispanic and female faculty are underrepresented in STEM fields. Conversely, the underrepresentation of Black, Hispanic and female faculty in non–STEM fields is not as pronounced and in some areas they are not underrepresented at all."[13]

Another study conducted by Nick Hazelberg of faculty diversity at doctoral granting universities revealed that between 2013 and 2017, Black tenured faculty increased by one-tenth of a percent or 4 percent of the total tenured faculty. At master's level universities, Black faculty representation was larger, comprising 5.6 percent of tenured faculty. However, progress is stagnant. During this same period, this group registered an even smaller increase of less than a tenth of a percent—or 0.07 percent. During this period, Hispanic and Latino tenured faculty grew by less than 1 percent (0.65) while faculty positions held by Asian Americans registered the biggest increase at doctoral-granting universities with an increase of 1.2 percent, comprising 12.8 percent of all tenured faculty.[14] Progress toward reducing racial disparities in faculty hiring and promotion remains tepid, not only for African Americans, but for Hispanic and Latino faculty as well.

When I returned from Vietnam in September 1970 and began graduate studies at Northwestern University, the broad outlines of federal policy regarding equality of opportunity that began with President Franklin Delano Roosevelt were expanding and exhibiting signs of progress, albeit uneven in higher education. What began as executive order and civil rights legislation were evolving into what came to be known as Affirmative Action. This is striking because this new approach emerged during the administration of President

Richard Nixon, a conservative Republican who won the election thanks to a so-called "Southern Strategy" aimed at the disaffection of Whites who traditionally voted as Democrats.

Affirmative Action had major implications for the federal government but also the public and private sectors and, colleges and universities that relied upon the federal government for financial support from Washington. Unequivocally, Affirmative Action, a forerunner or precursor to diversity initiatives, resulted in demographic shifts in enrollment and employment on college campuses. Arguably, the best evidence of this can be seen in the desegregation of American higher education. For example, in the 1950s and 1960s many, if not all, of the flagship public universities were exclusively White and male. By the late 1960s and early 1970s, this had begun to change thanks to court challenges and pressure from Washington, often with help from an activated United States National Guard in Alabama, Georgia, and Mississippi.

Fifty years ago, the vast majority of Black students were enrolled in Historically Black Colleges and Universities (HBCUs). Today, 90 percent of Black students attend predominantly White institutions or PWIs. Likewise, women comprise almost two-thirds of undergraduate enrollment on campuses across the country. Enrollment increases among Black and women students subsequently led to demands to increase the hiring of Black and female faculty and staff. The enrollment of other minority groups began to increase and, with it, demands to boost the hiring of Asian, Latino, and Native American faculty and staff.

At the dawn of the twenty-first century, diversity had replaced Affirmative Action as the central vehicle for increasing access and achieving equity in educational opportunity for a broad array of discriminated groups, including persons with disabilities and members of the LGBTQ community. Blacks and women have registered notable increases in enrollment, an undeniable indicator of progress to expanding diversity. Regrettably, the same cannot be said when it comes to faculty. In point of fact, there is a lot of unfinished business that calls for heightened interest and unqualified commitment.

## Faculty Diversity

Achieving faculty diversity is widely recognized as critical to organizational success. An *American Council on Education Report* in 2019 concluded that "Conversations on diversity in higher education often focus solely on student diversity, overlooking the importance of diversity among faculty, staff, and leadership. This diversity is critical, both for the effective management of the institutions, given research has shown that diverse companies are more productive and innovative."[15] While diversity may be increasing in higher education, it is important to describe in what ways. It may be helpful to examine the antecedents to current efforts to diversity and inclusion. Doing so will illuminate the gradual, but certain evolution from affirmative action, to what is now called diversity and inclusion; and equally important, its implications for the future with respect to race and ethnicity. Understanding the shift from affirmative action/equal employment opportunity (AA/EEO) to diversity and inclusion is emblematic of the choices and harsh realities decision-makers must confront in order to meaningfully address concerns pertaining to equity in the workplace.

In a *Harvard Business Review* article published more than three decades ago, Roosevelt Thomas, a leading proponent of affirmative action, predicted its demise. It would be replaced, he argued, by diversity in recognition of the fact that the nation's workforce was increasingly composed of "minorities, immigrants, and women."[16] Thomas' prediction has come to pass. Affirmative action/equal employment opportunity, originally designed to combat employment discrimination against African Americans, broadened its focus in order to meet workforce demands and competition in the marketplace. This is how Thomas described the situation:

American corporations are scrambling, doing their best to become more adaptable, to compete more successfully for markets and labor, foreign and domestic, and to attract all the talent they can find.[17]

Once a leading advocate for affirmative action, Thomas later concluded it was time to abandon an approach he believed was an "artificial, transitional intervention, intended to give managers a chance to correct an imbalance, an injustice, a mistake."[18] This was a major paradigm shift, but one that was in many ways more palatable to executives who were never comfortable with affirmative action from the start. To be sure, affirmative action had its supporters since the concept was first introduced during World War II, when President Franklin Delano Roosevelt came under enormous pressure from civil rights leaders to desegregate the armed forces and end discrimination in the war production industry. Roosevelt relented on the latter and it was his successor, President Harry Truman, in 1948, who issued Executive Order 9981 to desegregate the armed services.

The road to affirmative action was long, arduous and hard-fought. Abandoning it would not be easy, particularly since it was spawned by the civil rights movement. In tracing its history Erin Kelly and Frank Dobbin found that after Truman's edict, the next substantive move was President John F. Kennedy's executive order 10925, which required federal contractors to end discrimination "through affirmative action."[19]

In a very detailed and incisive analysis, Kelly and Dobbin trace the rise and fall of affirmative action from the 1960s to the 1990s. The role of the federal government in promoting AA/EEO is unassailable, just as it was successful in desegregating the armed services. The election of Ronald Reagan in 1980 presaged retrenchment, however. This should not have come as a surprise, since Reagan launched his campaign for president in Philadelphia, Mississippi, the town where three civil rights workers were tortured and slain in 1964. Kelly and Dobbin wrote that the election of Ronald Reagan resulted in reduced support and enforcement of AA/EEO, an attitude that continued into the administration of President Bill Clinton.

A key factor in the shift is attributed to a report commissioned by the Reagan administration's Department of Labor. Entitled Workforce 2000, the report was the handiwork of the Hudson Institute, a conservative think tank. Unequivocally, it laid the groundwork for abandoning affirmative action in favor of diversity management.

> The report outlined anticipated changes in the business environment, such as the globalization of markets, the growth of the service sector, technological advances, and demographic shifts in the labor force. Workforce 2000 projected that minorities and women would become an even larger share of the labor force. Two of the six "challenges" identified in the report were "reconciling the needs of women, work and families" and "integrating Blacks and Hispanics fully into the labor market."[20]

By the 1990s, AA/EEO specialists had imbibed the new concoction and charted a new course as diversity managers touting the importance of achieving the needs and fulfilling the expectations of American business and industry. AA/EEO managers reimagined their roles and now fashioned themselves as diversity experts. Consequently, by the early 1990s as M.L. "Wheeler noted, diversity initiatives had been adopted by 70 percent of Fortune 50 companies."[21] The die was cast. Affirmative action, which sought to address employment discrimination primarily against African Americans, had shifted its focus to diversity and inclusion. Opposition from the Reagan administration, coupled with Supreme Court decisions, resulted in a "new diversity management paradigm [that] incorporated many popular AA/EEO practices, but it did not include the most controversial Affirmative Action measures."[22]

In light of the foregoing, it is prudent to question whether diversity and inclusion policies and practices augur well for the recruitment and retention of African American faculty. Under AA/EEO generally, African Americans were viewed as the major victims of racial discrimination. Diversity and inclusion policies and practices are designed to increase access to women and racial minorities. Since this approach is intentionally diffuse and broad-based rather than targeted, it is likely to be less effective in recruiting and retaining African Americans specifically. Recent data on faculty employment by race suggest that the shift toward diversity in the future does not bode well for a significant increase in Black faculty. Greater emphasis on hiring executive level diversity and inclusion officers does not seem to help. Such positions are ubiquitous on nearly every university or college campus. Many cover a broad array of duties ranging from recruitment and hiring to sexual assault, hate, speech, and LGBTQ issues. Diversity officers span positions from deans and directors to vice presidents at some of the large research universities. According to economist and newspaper columnist Walter Williams,

> Penn State University's Office of Vice Provost for Educational Equity employs 66 staff members. The University of Michigan currently employs a diversity staff of 93 full-time diversity administrators, officers, ... executive assistants, administrative assistants, analysts, and coordinators.[23]

In far too many instances highly paid diversity and inclusion experts oversee activities that sometimes produce questionable results. If Black faculty are genuinely committed to increasing and retaining their number they must be vigilant and ensure that broad-based diversity and inclusion policies and procedures do not overlook them and their interests. There can be no substitute for intentionality. An absence of vigilance and intentional leadership will likely result in a decline of African American faculty and staff, as the agenda of other interest groups advance under the aegis of diversity and inclusion. The wisdom of the great abolitionist Frederick Douglass, eloquently expressed in 1857, is as instructive today as it was then:

> If there is no struggle there is no progress. Those who profess to favor freedom and yet deprecate agitation, are men who want crops without plowing up the ground, they want rain without thunder and lightning.

They want the ocean without the awful roar of its many waters.... Power concedes nothing without a demand. It never did and it never will.[24]

For two decades I held senior executive positions at major universities. These schools provided a unique vantage point from which to observe institutional commitment and progress toward racial equality, particularly increasing the number of Black faculty and staff. I saw firsthand the degree of genuine interest in attacking the problem. Issuing platitudes is easier than decisive action. The results show for themselves—and they are abysmally deficient.

Between 1993 and 2011, Daryl Smith, a leading expert on diversity in higher education, in a *Review of National Higher Education Data*, found that despite increases by race and gender during this period, by and large, faculty remained overwhelmingly White.[25]

Smith notes that between 1993 and 2011 faculty diversity increased numerically and percentage-wise among Whites, Blacks, Asian Americans, Pacific Islanders, Latinos, and American Indians/ Alaska Natives. Also, in each racial and ethnic group women faculty outpaced the growth of male faculty.[26]

Over the course of my career that spans more than four decades there has been progress but it has been minimal and slow, even halting. I long to be the eternal optimist but realism intrudes. Two recent publications validate my skepticism.

The first is a report by McKinsey and Company, one of the nation's leading consulting firms. In a study entitled "Racial and Ethnic Equity in Higher Education" McKinsey found that

88 percent of not-for-profit colleges and universities have full-time faculties that are less diverse than the U.S. population as of 2020. That number rises to 99 percent for institutions defined as R1 (i.e., the most intensive research ones). Progress in diversifying full-time faculty ranks to match the total population over the past decade has been negligible; it would take more than 1,000 years at the current pace to reach parity for all not-for-profit institutions. (R1 institutions will never reach parity at current rates.) When looking at both

faculty and students, few institutions are racially representative of the country; only 11 percent of not-for-profit institutions and 1 percent of R1 institutions are.[27]

The second publication is an article by Professor Mariappan Jawaharlal who expressed skepticism about the efficacy of diversity, equity and inclusion (DEI) activities. While acknowledging that many such programs may be well-intentioned, he argues rather convincingly based on data from the National Science Foundation that

> unfortunately, DEI initiatives have become prime examples of feel-good activities that sadly, will not lead to tangible results, especially in science, technology, engineering, and mathematics fields.[28]

Rather than simply bemoan the problem, I recommend the following:

1. Build partnerships with HBCUs and Hispanic-serving institutions. Close to 30 percent of Blacks who earned a doctorate in a STEM field (science, technology, engineering, and mathematics) completed their undergraduate degree at an HBCU,
2. Expand the pool of potential doctorates through financial support to undergraduates for research and mentorship programs; and
3. Create or expand engagements with local K–12 school systems.

Although these strategies are aimed at increasing diversity in the STEM areas, they are applicable to all areas of higher education.

Throughout my elementary and high school years a constant mantra of my teachers was "where there is a will there is a way." I continue to believe this to be true. When presidents and governing boards decide to be as intentional about recruiting and retaining Black faculty and staff as they are about recruiting student-athletes, then and only then will we see meaningful change.

## Faculty Diversity in Virginia

My academic career began in 1973. A lot has changed since then and undeniable progress has occurred. Still, much work remains. In

Virginia, where I spent several years of my career, faculty diversity at public universities mirrors the people nationally.

Faculty diversity at Virginia's research universities has improved in the last decade. Black faculty comprise 3.8 percent of Virginia Tech, 4.7 percent at the University of Virginia and 7.3 percent at Virginia Commonwealth University. The most noticeable increases have occurred among Asian American faculty, a trend consistent with national patterns. There are twice as many Asian American faculty as Black faculty at Virginia's research universities: University of Virginia 11.2 percent; Virginia Commonwealth University 15.3 percent; and Virginia Tech 16.2 percent.

Virginia's experience regarding faculty diversity in higher education is hardly unique. It is easy to be skeptical about permanent change. When it comes to confronting harsh realities on diversity issues, too often Black faculty are expected to do the heavy lifting.

Promotion and tenure committees often need diversity training. Faculty generally may be unaware of their own cultural biases and stereotypes expecting Black faculty to entertain or "lighten up and not be so serious."

Any improvement in an institution's diversity efforts must be intentional. The overrepresentation of Black faculty in lower paying professions (education, social work, etc.) rather than the so-called STEM areas is also a challenge that must be met with intentionality.

As a longtime observer of policies designed to address systemic racism in American society, I admit to a degree of skepticism about the latest permutation generally labeled "diversity." Diversity, equity and inclusion (DEI) initiatives should be met with caution because they often compromise and create challenges to programs designed to support the advancement of Black faculty particularly, in favor of gender and geographic considerations. In short, diversity can become so elastic that it can fit almost any definition resulting in diminishing its intended goals.

There is considerable work to be done; it will only be accomplished with determination and resolve. Skepticism aside, the widespread protests following the murder of George Floyd largely characterized by diverse participation offered a glimmer of hope for a better tomorrow. The optimism and fervor for change is wavering as the tide of conservatism is on the uptick. Several states are implementing legislation against what they describe as "wokeism" and "critical race theory." Diversity is under attack with shameless abandon with no relief in sight.

There is one more tidbit of information worthy of comment and that pertains to Black faculty at Virginia's HBCUs. Throughout their many years of segregated existence, HBCUs enjoyed a monopoly on faculty and students. Desegregation of higher education led to major disruptions in that model, resulting in huge enrollment declines at HBCUs today.

There are signs of slippage among faculty as well. Between 1993 and 2017, Black faculty at HBCUs lost ground, falling from 64 percent to 58 percent. During this period, Asian American faculty at HBCUs increased from 8 percent to 13 percent while White faculty held steady at 25–26 percent of positions. The June 2023 Supreme Court decision that struck down affirmative action will likely adversely affect the recruitment of Black students, particularly at elite colleges and universities with highly selective admissions policies and criteria. Some schools have already signaled that they intend to find creative ways to achieve diversity including the abandonment of legacy admissions. It remains to be seen, however, if the same level of attention and fervor will be given to the recruitment of Black faculty where many already find themselves in a precarious situation.

## CHAPTER ELEVEN

# The Way Forward

If meaningful change is to occur, Black faculty and staff must lead the way. Albeit true that we should not be responsible for solving a problem we did not create, the simple truth is that if we don't act as history shows, nothing will change. As Frederick Douglass exhorted there can be no progress without struggle. We must continue to probe, prod and protest to demand the attention of institutional leadership. The role of one such organization at Virginia Commonwealth University provides an example.

The role of VCU's Black Education Association (BEA) in the recruitment and retention of Black faculty is indisputable. The BEA and other single-focused organizations like it on campuses across the country are essential to the continued role African American faculty and staff must play in the future. When the BEA was created in 1970, just two years following the founding of VCU, it could not have imagined how important it would be to Black faculty and staff, the university writ large, the local community, state government, and particularly, to higher education. In a brief history of BEA, Camisha Jones writes:

> Early BEA leaders saw the organization as a vehicle for providing cultural awareness programming, professional development activities, and opportunities for minorities to be a part of VCU's decision-making processes, increased collaboration between VCU and Richmond's Black community and better communication between Black students, faculty, staff and administrators.[1]

The BEA was born of necessity. Its origins were framed in a period of racial discord and discrimination, anti-war sentiment, a fledgling university administration and general uncertainty about the level of legislative and public support, given its recent existence compared to other well-established public universities in Virginia. Simply put, the Black Education Association emerged in fraught circumstances but since its founding, it has played a pivotal role in supporting the aspirations of Black faculty and staff as well as students. There is no doubt that VCU is better because of the BEA.

In a brief history of the association, Jean Garrett, one of BEA's early members, expressed doubt that VCU was aware of how beneficial BEA was to the university's success:

> For instance, BEA played a critical role in the recruitment and retention of Black students. Members who were administrators traveled across the state to help recruit Black students and offered academic and general support to enrolled students. Because of mentoring offered by BEA members, Garrett credits the organization for the founding of the Black medical students organization. Additionally, BEA funded and organized an overnight gathering for the students to connect with Black doctors and dentists. The BEA members assisted students interested in medical careers to apply to medical and dental school. Garrett believes there are many Black students during that period who would not have stayed at VCU or been as successful, while enrolled, if it were not for the efforts of BEA members.[2]

Truly, if the BEA did not exist, it would have had to be invented. Its advocacy within VCU, and at the state and federal levels was critical throughout its history. From pushing for divestment in South Africa, to urging renewal of the Virginia Plan for Equal Opportunity in State Supported Institutions of Higher Education, to ensuring representation on search committees for faculty and administrators, to creating the Office of Multi-Cultural Student Affairs, and to creating the Faculty Assistance and Mentorship Enhancement program (FAME) unequivocally, the BEA has been critical to the advancing the mission of VCU. As the BEA has aimed for effectiveness, its ability to build support among Richmond's Black leaders, including state legislators, local elected officials, local and state government officials, and civic and professional groups, cannot be overstated. BEA and other faculty and staff advocacy of its type should not be taken for granted. Let me elaborate further.

If we have learned anything from our history, it is that those who do not know it may be doomed to repeat it. Yes, we've made progress, but much work remains. Battles have been won, but the fight is far from over. In the words of the freedom fighter Jonas Savimbi, "A luta continua," the struggle continues.

Although it did not do it alone, the BEA has a proven track record of success in the recruitment and retention of Black faculty and staff and students as well. If it is to maintain its effectiveness or even hold its own, it must accelerate its efforts. Similarly, for other colleges and universities in Virginia and across the country, if there is no organized effort to promote the recruitment and retention of Black faculty and staff, their numbers will continue to decline. With the loss of Black faculty and staff, one can expect that their interests and concerns will get lost in the quest for what is now called diversity and inclusion.

While organized leadership by Black faculty and staff is necessary it is not sufficient to achieve racial and ethnic diversity in higher education. Solid commitment by institutional leadership including support from governing boards is absolutely essential as a report from the nation's leading organizations on governance makes clear:

> Governing boards have a moral, a fiduciary, and an educational responsibility to provide leadership on issues of justice, equity, and inclusion in higher education. The business and financial imperatives for these efforts are equally compelling. Failure to address these issues poses serious threats to institutional integrity, brand, and mission relevance.[3]

Faculty, staff and students—indeed, all stakeholders and constituencies—must know that the president has the solid backing of the board in achieving diversity, racial and ethnic diversity in higher education.

## Chapter Twelve

# The Future of Historically Black Colleges and Universities

For more than fifty years, starting with my undergraduate years at Grambling College, I have maintained a keen and abiding interest in Historically Black Colleges and Universities, commonly referred to as HBCUs. I have studied HBCUs as an area of scholarly interest, especially on matters pertaining to leadership and governance. Their importance to this nation, to higher education, and indeed to people all over the world cannot be overstated. The narrative does not end here, however.

We speak of HBCUs as iconic institutions in almost reverential terms, and for good reason. HBCUs have always enrolled more low-income students than White or majority schools. This singular fact is worthy of more than passing reference. HBCUs almost single-handedly created the Black middle-class, producing teachers, ministers, doctors, engineers, scientists, engineers and entrepreneurs. While this is generally known and appreciated among direct beneficiaries, African Americans particularly, it is validated in findings from a recent report from the Rutgers Center for Minority Serving Institutions. It found that:

> Nearly 70% of HBCU students attain at least middle-class incomes and most low-income HBCU students can expect to improve their long-term economic position.... Xavier University of Louisiana and Tuskegee University, for example, achieve higher mobility than any other HBCU.[1]

---

In an era when diversity and inclusion give the appearance of heralding a new millennium, America's HBCUs have led by example since their inception. The eminent historian John Hope Franklin, himself a product of Fisk University, in a speech entitled "Higher Education and the World Community," given at Brooklyn College, characterized Black colleges as "America's multiracial and multicultural pioneers":

> Whether the institution had a conscious and deliberate plan, such as Hampton Institute, to provide education for Negroes, Indians and Hawaiians, or a less overt arrangement, such as Howard, to educate all who could come, black colleges early became the models for the training of persons of the most diverse racial, cultural or even national backgrounds. There was no presumption of such institutions that barriers to learning ... existed or that education was not an effective instrument for solving the most difficult problems imaginable. Such institutions, I argued, were essentially optimistic, expressing through their curriculum, their faculty, and their students a belief in their mission to improve the human condition, anywhere and everywhere. Few organizations in this country during the nineteenth and early twentieth centuries had attempted this.[2]

Equality of opportunity is in the DNA of America's Black colleges and universities. As Gabrielle Edgcomb points out, because of rampant anti–Semitism and outright quotas, many Jews found it difficult to gain admission to elite colleges and universities including medical, dental and law schools. The Howard University College of Medicine was one that did not discriminate.[3]

The contributions of HBCUs are at once immeasurable and unassailable. They are iconic institutions with a vaunted legacy that is without comparison. It is hard to imagine what the United States, indeed the world, would be like were it not for Black colleges and universities. That is because HBCUs are considerably more than institutions of higher learning. Some are rural and others are urban. Some are private or independent, owing to their denominational ties, but most are public. In all instances, they are repositories of history, culture, art, and politics. On HBCU campuses one will find buildings with distinctive architecture, libraries and museums that house prized works by African American muralists, artists, writers, composers, sculptors and poets. Their libraries contain intellectual property—books, journals, original research produced by African American scholars, dating back to their founding after Reconstruction.

Every Black college campus has a story to tell: Hampton University's Emancipation Oak; the monument to the United States Colored Troops who founded Lincoln University in Missouri; Jubilee Hall at Fisk University, named in honor of the famed choral group that travelled the globe to raise money for the school; or the many HBCU campuses, too numerous to mention, where buildings were constructed and grounds were landscaped and maintained with student labor. Long before the recruitment of international students became popular, Howard University was on the vanguard making a difference, again, almost singlehandedly, recruiting and enrolling students from across the globe. Many would rise to positions of leadership, helping to topple colonial regimes.

The distinguished historian Rayford Logan describes in intimate detail how the history of Howard University was always committed to opening its doors to international students. Logan writes that during the 1966–67 school year Howard enrolled 1667 students from Africa, the Caribbean, Central America, Europe, the Far East, near and Middle East, North America, and South America.[4] Also, in the twentieth century, when many American colleges and universities systematically applied admission quotas, Howard University's professional schools—namely, medicine, dentistry and law—had no problem with enrolling Jews.

Since their founding, HBCUs have been noted for providing opportunities for higher education to disenfranchised citizens even though their tax dollars supported public colleges and universities that denied them access. A recent report of the Association of Governing Boards of Universities and Colleges (AGB) sums up the importance of HBCUs as follows:

HBCUs can be credited with enabling African-Americans to achieve upward mobility that had long been denied them, engendering the middle class—the physicians, lawyers, scientists, engineers, educators, business leaders and others who achieved success within and alongside predominantly white professions. HBCUs can also be credited with producing many of the leaders of the American Civil Rights Movement, which sought to end the economic, political and cultural oppression of African-Americans.[5]

While acknowledging the key role HBCUs have played in higher education and society, the report describes conditions that demand immediate attention. Their future, the AGB report argues, "will depend on strong governance, strategic leadership and robust financial health."[6]

The desegregation of higher education has had a discernible adverse impact on HBCUs. As recently as the 1960s, the overwhelming majority of African Americans were enrolled at HBCUs. Today, 90 percent of African Americans are enrolled at White colleges and universities. While it is true that HBCUs compose only 3 percent of higher education institutions yet produce 16 percent of college graduates, they are experiencing enormous pressure on several fronts.

For most of their existence HBCUs enjoyed an almost pure monopoly on the recruitment of Black students and faculty. Today, HBCUs must compete not only with White public and private universities and colleges but also two-year colleges, for-profit universities, and vocational and technical schools designed to equip graduates for the workforce.

In order to compete more effectively, HBCUs must do more than seek survival. Instead, they must be intentional about securing a sustainable future. The 2019 AGB report offers this blunt recommendation: "The sustainability of HBCUs rests on three factors: a new business model, cogent leadership, and sound governance."[7]

These recommendations, although simple and straightforward, must be taken seriously. Regrettably, if history is any guide, it is difficult to be sanguine on this matter. Higher education experts, including outstanding former presidents and leaders of HBCUs, have been sounding the alarm for decades. The former chancellor of North Carolina Central University, Albert Whiting, in an aptly titled book, *Guardians of the Flame*, written thirty years ago and based on in-depth interviews with twenty HBCU presidents and presidents emeriti, conveyed a deep and passionate concern that HBCUs might become "a relic of the past—a vanishing symbol of a valiant struggle for knowledge outside the mainstream?"[8]

There can be no gainsaying the fact that HBCUs are at an inflection point; however, they are needed now more than ever. Of particular concern is the widening gender imbalance on nearly all Black college campuses. Although this is also true for White colleges and universities, it is worse at HBCUs where it is not uncommon to find women comprising 50 to 60 percent of the first-year class. Two key factors explain this disparity. One has to do with the comparatively low high school graduation rate of African American males. According to the most recent data available, only 59 percent of Black males nationwide graduated from high school. In the Detroit public schools, only 20 percent of Black males graduated on time. It is hard to enroll in college without a high school diploma.

The second key factor is more historic and cultural. When opportunities to attend college first opened, female Black students from rural or farm areas were more likely to enroll in college over Black males who were needed to help with production. Additionally, and equally important, Black parents were determined that their daughters would receive an education so that they would not have to work as domestics and be subjected to the predatory behavior of White men. John Hope Franklin offers this personal affirmation:

> During the years of Reconstruction the newly freed father was more anxious to educate his daughters and place them in positions beyond the reach of white men who, all too often with cause, were suspected of being sexual predators. With this in mind, my maternal grandfather sent all his daughters, including my mother, and none of his sons to college. Meanwhile, it was only because the white headmistress of the preparatory school in the Indian Territory saw much

promise in my father that she insisted my paternal grandfather send him to college. Thus, my father became the only educated male of his siblings.[9]

Additionally, in much of the South, education for Black students stopped at the eighth grade. Parents who wanted their children to further their education often had to send them to a neighboring town or city, or out of state to live with relatives in order to earn a high school diploma. Katherine Johnson, the famed NASA scientist whose life and career are depicted in the book *Hidden Figures*, and in a movie by the same name, was among the fortunate ones. In order that Katherine and her siblings could graduate high school, her parents moved 425 miles away from their home in White Sulphur Springs, West Virginia, to another town because education for Black children stopped at the sixth grade.

The road to Black progress has been paved by education and it has occurred despite seemingly impossible odds. Untold sacrifices and immeasurable amounts of blood, sweat, and tears have accompanied every inch and mile of advancement at every level. The spotlight is on the present generation to ensure that progress continues and that HBCUs contribute all that they can. A huge responsibility rests on the shoulders of HBCU leaders. In particular, there are several critical areas that deserve the attention of HBCU presidents and governing boards. They are based on decades of personal experience and observation along with many years of professional consultation. These recommendations and insights are offered in the spirit of helpful advice to anyone interested and committed to the sustainability of HBCUs.

Black colleges and universities are often described as under-resourced, enrolling a disproportionate number of students from low-income families and the first in their family to attend college, all of which is generally accurate. However, as badly as these institutions need more funding, several impediments to their success have little to nothing to do with money. Rather, they pertain to management and organizational issues that are often unrelated to finances. Mainly, the obstacles to success have to do with organizational culture and resistance to change, sometimes even in the face of incontrovertible evidence of the need for urgent action.

The threats that imperil the future of HBCUs are well-known and verified across public and private colleges and universities. They are as follows:

- Declining enrollment
- Institutional and board leadership
- Reductions in state funding
- Obsolete business model
- Uncertain federal funding
- A dearth of future leadership talent
- Inadequate financial support from alumni
- Inadequate financial support for intercollegiate athletics

These are not new concerns. In point of fact, several were raised in *Guardians of the Flame* published thirty years ago and also more recently.[10] What is lacking is a failure to acknowledge the urgency of the situation and a commitment to courageous, intentional leadership by chief executives and governing boards. The desire or will to act is of paramount importance. Listed below are five KEY AREAS that if properly addressed, can lead to a sustainable path for HBCUs. In each instance, effective board governance is critically important.

ACCOUNTABILITY. It is a truism that a university or college can never be better than its board. As higher education has changed to adjust to new realities, so also have boards stepped up to meet them. Leadership in the presidency is important, but also is board leadership. Effective board governance does not occur by happenstance; it is achieved with intentionality. Effective board governance occurs when a board has the right members, the board concentrates on the right issues and board members engage in the right way among themselves and others. As well, the board takes the long view, does not get in the weeds but instead focuses on sustainability.

Creating a sustainable path for a university or college cannot happen without creating a culture of accountability and ensuring that it is a priority for the president, the chief executive's direct reports, and subordinate levels of administration throughout the organization. It must be inherent in the culture of the organization. In order to achieve organizational goals and fulfill its mission, every organization must rely upon and insist on the allocation of rewards and penalties through some type of formal institutional structure or system. This is a basic tenet of organizational structure. The noted organization theorist Amatai Etzioni describes it this way:

> Most organizations most of the time cannot rely on most of their participants to carry out their assignments voluntarily, to have internalized their obligations. The participants need to be supervised, the supervisors themselves need supervision, and so on, all the way to the top of the organization.[11]

In his best-selling book *The 7 Habits of Highly Effective People,* Stephen Covey writes that accountability is necessary in order to "Set up standards of performance that will be used in evaluating the results and the specific times when reporting and evaluation take place."[12] Accountability is absolutely essential to achieving organizational goals. It must permeate every facet of the organization, must be embraced enthusiastically, and should become a natural way of getting things done. Accountability starts and ends with the governing board. As AGB's president Henry Stoever pointed out recently, "The most important principle of strategic board leadership is realizing that the board is accountable for everything that happens or fails to happen within the institution or foundation ... it is critical for board members to recognize that their primary duty is to be accountable for the institution's long-term reputation and vitality."[13]

Accountability starts and ends with the governing board. A board, whether public or private, has fiduciary duties that are inescapable and the ability to ensure a sustainable future for the institution rests in its hands. These include fulfilling the mission through oversight of educational quality, financial sufficiency, accreditation, campus safety, and security, facilities planning and management, and risk management. Some leaders believe they can achieve goals through autocracy—that is, through a top-down leadership style where authority and decision-making are concentrated in the hands of the president. Unfortunately, some HBCUs continue to operate this way with tacit or explicit board approval. This approach may have worked in certain institutions in the past, but it has produced mixed results in terms of long-term success or creation of a path toward sustainability.

In light of the harsh conditions of segregation and the racial antipathy toward their existence at the time of their founding, "Black college presidents acquired a near god-like status on their campus and in their community. They did not brook opposition and recalcitrance of any type was not tolerated."[14] In far too many instances, autocracy has resulted in a lack of board fulfillment of fiduciary duties, diminished importance of the role of faculty in shared governance and silence among key stakeholders such as faculty, students, and alumni. This is too high a price to pay.

It is incumbent upon the governing board to recognize and embrace accountability as an essential part of their fiduciary duties. This begins with clear expectations of the president and his or her direct reports. To be effective, accountability must permeate every level in the organization and it must start and end with the governing board.

LEADERSHIP. As noted in the foregoing, leadership is absolutely essential to achieving sustainability for a college or university. The most important decision a board makes is the selection of a president. This is increasingly difficult however, as the pool of potential candidates is small and seemingly shrinking. Just as African American students and faculty have greater options today than previously existed, so do higher education leaders at all levels—presidents, vice presidents, deans and directors, etc. Because of a lack of due diligence on the part of governing boards, presidents, sometimes with multiple failures, have been hired nonetheless. The recycling of inept leadership can lead to disaster, particularly in the case of HBCUs where the margin of error is close to zero. A bad hiring decision in the hiring of a president can and has proved fatal to the future of some schools.

Board leadership is equally important, as increasingly boards must ensure that they have the right composition with the appropriate skills and backgrounds to do the board's work. A strong governance committee of the board can be helpful in determining the various needs of the board in key areas such as academic affairs, higher education finance, fundraising, marketing and branding, and information technology. Organizations require a certain type of leader at various stages of their history and development. Boards must be clear about existing conditions and challenges the institution is facing as well as expectations for the future in order to determine the type of leader it needs, when it launches a search.

ADAPTABILITY. Managing change is an ongoing challenge for institutions of higher education. If an organization is not moving forward it is standing still and probably losing ground. HBCUs are no different. Organizations are inherently conservative and inclined to maintain and preserve customs, norms, and traditions. HBCUs fit this pattern well. Yet we live in an era when change, much of it driven by technology, is omnipresent and irrepressible. If an organization is not changing, it is likely falling behind.

There are many examples of the inability to adapt to change in modern society, but one common frame of reference is the American automobile industry. At one time, Detroit, Michigan, was the center of automobile manufacturing. Scores of companies were in the automobile manufacturing business. Some were very good, actually, but for a variety of reasons simply could not survive the competition. During this golden age of the automobile three industry leaders emerged and dominated this sector for decades: General Motors

Corporation, the Ford Motor Company, and the Chrysler Corporation. General Motors (GM) emerged as pre-eminent among the Big Three, as they were then called.

The lessons of a failure of the automobile industry to adapt and innovate did not end there, however. The oil crisis of the early 1970s and increased sensitivity to fuel economy, the environment and safety led to the greater numbers of imported automobiles from Japan, Germany, and Britain, and the dominance of the Big Three, GM, Ford, and Chrysler, began to noticeably shrink. Throughout the twentieth century the Big Three essentially dominated the automobile market in the United States. Because of their success at home they also influenced global sales. General Motors was dominant among the Big Three and had 50 percent of the market share in the United States in the 1960s. By 2022 the Big Three's market share had been reduced to 17 percent. Even the luxury car market, once the exclusive preserve of Cadillac, followed by Lincoln and Imperial, has been replaced by Mercedes-Benz, BMW, and Lexus. Where once Chevrolet, Ford, and Plymouth ruled, Korean and Japanese marques like Toyota, Honda, Nissan, and Hyundai now prevail.

The automobile industry is but one example of how innovation has upended one sector of the American economy. There are others, from health care to airlines to agriculture. Change is omnipresent and higher education has not been immune to it. Since the 1980s, American universities and colleges have undergone tremendous change. To meet the competition, they have had to adapt and implement practices, often identified with business and industry. Terms that were once anathema in the academy like marketing, segmentation, retention, and return on investment, or ROI, are now commonplace.

In the realm of fundraising for example, historically a practice engaged in primarily by private or independent colleges and universities, today, more and more public or state-supported colleges and universities, are involved in capital campaigns. Almost daily, one reads about a major research university or a small liberal arts college launching a multi-million dollar or even multi-billion dollar campaign. Whereas originally the president was expected to be an academic leader, today's chief executive spends more than half of his or her time raising funds, a quest that seemingly never ends. And when fundraising isn't going on, considerable attention is given to friend-raising, which must precede the actual ask.

The competition in higher education is fierce. Traditional colleges and universities must compete with for-profit schools, two-year institutions, online universities and technical colleges. The increasing popularity in several states of "free tuition" programs to encourage enrollment at community colleges poses a serious threat to HBCUs, since many of them cater to the same applicant pool. Furthermore, the availability of dual degree programs that enable an enterprising high school student to earn an associate degree while simultaneously earning a diploma is difficult to ignore. While dual degree programs may pose a threat to HBCUs, they could also provide a steady source of recruitment through articulation agreements with two-year and four-year institutions as part of an intentional enrollment management strategy. The operative word is intentional. If HBCUs are to achieve sustainability they must adapt to shifting demands in the market. Because they no longer enjoy a monopoly on students and faculty, HBCUs must be willing to change and adapt. Opportunities to collaborate with two-year schools is but one example.

In order for it to be effective this strategy must be supported by HBCU presidents and governing boards. Faculty must be willing to take the time to meet with community college faculty colleagues to identify courses that are acceptable for transfer credit leading to a baccalaureate degree program. Provosts, deans, and department chairs at HBCUs must be willing to clear bureaucratic hurdles to ease the transfer process for community college students. These can be laborious time-consuming efforts but if done well, can produce huge benefits.

This is but one approach that can be part of a new business

model designed to achieve sustainability. Other aspects to which a new business model can respond relate to creating new degree programs that satisfy student and industry demands, improving the quality of student life, study abroad programs, internships, expanded extra-curricular and co-curricular programs, and improving campus facilities and amenities. Depending upon an institution's resources and appetite for change, these can be daunting, even overwhelming expectations, since as the 2019 AGB report notes, "within both public and private sectors, HBCU endowments lag behind those of non–HBCUs, by at least 70 percent."[15]

In keeping with their mission, HBCUs have always tried to ensure access and affordability for their students, many of whom are the first in their family to attend college and come from low-income backgrounds. HBCUs have produced amazing results despite underfunding. They have kept tuition low while distributing generous financial aid packages to students. This practice has been costly to the institutions, however, as it has caused them to operate on the margins financially, susceptible to almost any disruption in federal or state support. This was the case with changes in the Pell Grant and the Parent Plus Loan Program during the Obama administration that resulted in enrollment drops at several HBCUs. It was a scary prospect that should not be repeated. Another reason that HBCUs have operated on the financial margins is because many lack the ability to raise funds. Again, according to the Association of Governing Boards of Universities and Colleges, AGB, "some HBCUs have not developed the capacity to establish legacy endowments—both reliable and significant revenue streams for most four-year colleges and universities."[16]

It is important to acknowledge that HBCUs are not monolithic. Although most lack healthy endowments, some like Claflin University in South Carolina have been extraordinarily successful in fundraising. Thanks to the exceptional leadership of President Henry Tisdale and an effective governing board, Claflin completed a campaign in 2016 that raised $105 million, the largest in its history. For several years Claflin University has been the top-ranked HBCU in terms of alumni giving. The university's alumni giving rate increased from 43 percent in 2013 to 52.2 percent by the time the campaign ended. In addition to enthusiastic alumni support, strong executive and effective board leadership, the advantages of a stable presidency cannot be ignored.

President Tisdale served 25 years before retiring at the conclusion of the campaign. Investments in the advancement operation including enhanced technology and maximizing the uses of social media were also enormously helpful. Claflin University offers demonstrable proof that HBCUs can create successful fundraising activities. Improving an institution's finances enhances the likelihood of long-term viability. Accepting change and adapting to new ways of fundraising is difficult, but the benefits far outweigh the costs. Improving fundraising must be a key part of any change strategy.

Adopting a new business model may be the most sweeping change imaginable for Black colleges. An intentional, calculated set of actions are required to reset the future of HBCUs. As Jim Collins points out, "change for the sake of change is unwise." There must be a consistent rationale for change, an understanding of the reasons current practices exist and when to keep or change them.[17] It takes courage to raise difficult questions about practices and procedures that have been in place for many years. This may be especially hard in institutions where there is a propensity to hire alumni or others who wish to maintain the status quo. This is where board leadership is critical, even though boards themselves can sometimes find it difficult to change. In light of their fiduciary duties, boards must act in the best long-term interests of the institution nonetheless.

Leadership often means making tough decisions. It helps to have a board composed of talented, experienced individuals who are unafraid to confront harsh realities. Increasingly, because of the challenges boards are facing, there is greater emphasis on recruiting individuals who possess expertise in specific areas. The AGB has developed a sample board matrix for boards to consider in the recruitment of new members. This approach enables a board to be intentional about the specific skills required to create an effective governing board. For an institution of higher learning, these might include knowledge of the academy, higher education finance, marketing and branding, information technology and risk management. HBCUs must be intentional and strategic in building an effective board that is committed to institutional sustainability.

A critical success factor in this regard is the board chair and president relationship. These two individuals have the greatest influence on building an effective board. In effect, the board chair and the president are partners and thought leaders. They acknowledge that leadership of necessity resides in the governing board and the presidency, and in order to achieve institutional goals, they strive to foster collaboration. Terrence MacTaggart argues convincingly that the board–president partnership is best viewed within the context of what he calls, "enterprise leadership."

Creating a board–president partnership depends on understanding the fundamentals of the academy, and how it works but, also its own special character of board governance. Higher education governance is distinct and qualitatively different from corporate or nonprofit board governance and its members must understand how and why. Issues like promotion and tenure, intellectual property, academic freedom and shared governance are often uncommon on corporate boards. Universities with medical centers, teaching hospitals and research parks also require skills that governing boards must be intentional about recruiting for selected skills. Building an effective board cannot happen without a solid board chair-president partnership.

In order to sharpen the meaning, think of a college or university as a multi-faceted organization, composed of distinct but related units. Here is MacTaggart's basic argument: "Effective enterprise leaders of colleges and universities engage the academic community in the change process. They work actively with their governing board as trusted partners in developing strategies to strengthen the institution's financial base, its academic quality and effectiveness, and its reputation for value to students and society."[18]

INSULARITY. Another major hurdle for HBCUs to surmount is a tendency toward insularity, that is, a reluctance to engage the larger social, political, and economic environment in which they exist. Again, this is a generalization and its degree or extent will vary by institution. But it is real nonetheless and must be confronted head-on if HBCUs are to realize their full potential. This impediment to modernity does not require dollars and cents but intentional leadership and acknowledgment that institutions must have partners for progress. They must be integrally tied to their community so that local citizens, businesses, civic organizations, and philanthropists understand and appreciate the value they add to the city and the region.

In other words, the Black college or university, wherever it is located, wants to be embraced and respected so much that local support is genuine and solid. The insularity that is characteristic of many, if not most, HBCUs is both attitudinal and physical. It is also understandable given the circumstances of their founding. The origins of insularity date to the founding of HBCUs after the Civil War. Again, it is important to note that Black colleges and universities are not monolithic and that the degree of insularity or social isolation varies by institution.

The historical antecedents to insularity at HBCUs are well-known but rarely discussed possibly, because they are so closely tied to race, a topic that is almost always difficult to talk about. Racial segregation and antipathy toward the education of Blacks explain in the simplest terms the insularity of Black colleges and universities. From the onset of their creation overt threats to their existence were common. Many were located in rural areas partly because land was cheap, or because of specialized degree programs related to agricultural, industrial, or technical education. Some, no doubt, were built in pastoral settings on the premise that they would be "out of sight and out of mind." Whatever the rationale, the simple truth is that if HBCUs are to maximize their options and achieve their full potential they must find ways to increase their involvement in the communities they reside in, history notwithstanding. Insularity is deeply imbedded in the culture of many HBCUs, and it has been reinforced by presidential leadership over time.

Initially, the leaders of HBCUs were White men. They and the schools they led depended heavily on the financial support of White philanthropy. Educating Black students was acceptable as long as they stayed in their place. Eventually, Black presidents succeeded White presidents, but the leadership model did not change for the most part.

In other words, Black college presidents were expected to provide conservative leadership. They understood the responsibility to keep students and faculty in line and to maintain order so as not to threaten racial customs and norms. The prevalence of insularity is cited several times in considerable detail in a very thoughtful and incisive book about "refugee scholars" who found employment at HBCUs during World War II.

> As Edgcomb describes, "Living conditions varied greatly in the urban colleges from those removed from towns and cities. At the urban ones, the refugee scholars found housing in the surrounding areas. Some campuses, while adjacent to a town, had no contact with the totally segregated life there. At Talladega, Alabama, the college is adjacent to the town of Talladega, but separate from it. Thus, the faculty lived on campus, where there were schools from pre-school through high school for all faculty children, black and white. Needless to say, the local townspeople viewed them with hostility."[19]

The fact that many HBCUs were established in major cities including Atlanta, Baltimore, Memphis, and Washington, D.C., did not necessarily alter the tendency toward insularity. Of necessity, this must change and the reasons are simple and straightforward: social, political, and philanthropic support. Increasingly, whether public or private, colleges and universities are relying upon private fundraising to remain competitive. This requires getting out of one's comfort zone and cultivating new relationships as well as building on existing ones.

First, however, there must be a cultivation of relationships with key stakeholders in the community: leaders in local government, businesses, hospitals, civic organizations, people who can make connections that lead to political and financial support. A selective approach to opening the campus to events and activities can reap infinite benefits. Athletic events are one tried and true way of generating enthusiastic support for the hometown team. Additionally, HBCUs are great repositories of history, art and culture. Their libraries and archives hold valuable books and monographs containing original research by some of the nation's leading African American scholars. Their museums feature valuable paintings, sculptures and murals by noted African Americans. Creating opportunities to expand access to the campus can lead to improved town-gown relations, while showcasing the institution's importance to the city, region, and state. These activities create opportunities for building relationships that can lead to long-term support.

Colleges and universities in general are major assets in their communities. Presidents and governing boards must figure out ways to take advantage of the multiple ways they can leverage their presence. For example, colleges and universities can partner with local governments in areas such as campus safety and transportation. There are many overlapping interests given the porous nature of most urban campuses. Many institutions have inter-jurisdictional agreements with local police departments. These pacts are mutually beneficial and for colleges or universities with limited policing resources, they are essential to ensuring a safe environment for students, faculty and staff. Additional areas of partnership center around transportation, housing, and economic development.

The potential expansion of a campus requires good relations and partnerships with local leaders and government officials. Similarly, local governments and businesses may see potential benefits from involvement with college or university degree programs related to workforce development. Finally, because institutions of higher education are natural assets, it is in their enlightened self-interest to occasionally conduct a study to ascertain their economic impact on the city and the region. The spending power of students and employees, the spin-offs from new construction and campus renovations, as well as the attraction of alumni and others to athletic and cultural events is huge and should be measured and understood. HBCUs should take advantage of these opportunities but in order to maximize their options, they must eliminate a tendency toward insularity.

Ideally, the local HBCU wants to be viewed as special, as an asset that citizens feel proud of and enthusiastic about supporting. In order to succeed, this approach must be intentional and strategic. Additionally, it must have support of the governing board, the president, and other key stakeholders including faculty, staff, students, and alumni. That is critical because in light of the racial history of HBCUs there will likely always be skeptics who are understandably reluctant to chart a new course, even if the benefits outweigh the costs.

ROMANTICISM. Black colleges and universities are iconic but in some ways they are also idyllic, conjuring notions of an intellectual and social life not found on a White campus. There is some truth to this perception. It is grounded in occurrences unique to HBCUs, such as the emergence of the Harlem Renaissance and the civil rights movement, for example. HBCUs as educational institutions have also served as incubators for the social, economic, scientific, and political progress of Black people since their inception. Of course, there is much to be justifiably proud about but we should not become so enamored of the past that we fail to build on our extraordinary accomplishments against insuperable odds. This is what I refer to as romanticism—idealized notions about what existed in the past without recognizing the need to visualize a new future.

Initially, Black colleges and universities were available only to a privileged few, offering a lifestyle and a set of opportunities unimaginable for the masses of Black people. In their avowed tribute to HBCUs, *I'll Find a Way or Make One*, Juan Williams and Duane Ashley described several scenarios where African American students and faculty revolted against oppressive rules in order to create a culture that reflected their needs and aspirations, rather than the White men who led them.[20]

The Black college student protest movement did not begin with the Student Nonviolent Coordinating Committee (SNCC) in the 1960s. In the early twentieth century, Black students and faculty launched aggressive campaigns to remove White presidents and replace them with Black presidents. Thus, Mordecai W. Johnson, in 1926, became the first African American to lead Howard University. John Hope was appointed Atlanta University's first African American president in 1929. Horace Mann Bond became the first African American president of his alma mater, Lincoln University (Pennsylvania), in 1945, and in 1946, Charles S. Johnson, a highly regarded author and scholar, assumed the presidency of Fisk University. These appointments were the direct result of agitation by Black students, faculty, and alumni and, without a doubt, they engendered enormous excitement and pride. In each instance, the new presidents were men of considerable achievement.

HBCUs are also social organizations, and because initially large numbers of students came from homes where college attendance was expected, perceptions about what college life was like and what it could lead to started to change. The noted sociologist, Charles S. Johnson, in *The Negro College Graduate*, noted that whereas "previous generations of Black students viewed college as a means to social and economic elevation, moving them from the ranks of the lower class to the middle-class, college students of the 1920s, often already defined themselves as middle-class."[21]

Consequently, some students may have focused undue attention on social status. Under these circumstances, membership in certain social clubs and Greek letter organizations, family wealth and skin tone, assumed a vaunted and differentiated role. Williams and Ashley offer this point of view:

> The manifestation of these growing class distinctions could be seen in the assuming nature of many HBCU graduates. College quickly was becoming a place where career and social connections were made, spouses were found, and the folly of youth encouraged—if not by the faculty and administration, then certainly by the students themselves. Academic achievement was, but one of many—and not even among the most important—criteria that determined social standing and future success.[22]

One could argue that these issues are not unique to HBCUs. College life has many parts and learning is not the exclusive preserve of the classroom. The social aspects of college life notwithstanding, the single-handed role HBCUs have played in producing not only outstanding individual leaders, but entire generations of leaders are undeniable. For example, no university can rival the Howard University Law School in the production of outstanding civil rights attorneys. Howard and Meharry medical schools are without peer in the production of physicians and dentists. Spelman College is incomparable in the production of graduates who earn a Ph.D. in the sciences, and Xavier University (Louisiana) is in a class by itself in graduating students who complete medical school. Although the track record of HBCUs is clear, there can be no resting on laurels.

So yes, HBCUs are iconic and special, but it is equally important that their value as institutions of higher education is unquestioned and continues to be strengthened. Black colleges and universities must not be romanticized to the point that they are viewed as sacrosanct and therefore, do not need to be improved. HBCUs coexist with hundreds of institutions of higher education with whom they must compete. There can be no sense of entitlement simply because of their historic and unique origin and character. One should not expect that an HBCU must compromise standards for historic, social or cultural reasons. An HBCU without a strong endowment must always be careful about admissions decisions that could exacerbate financial stress and possibly lead to disaster. The social and cultural aspects of the Black college experience are extremely important, but HBCUs for all their iconic value must not be romanticized to the point that critical success factors, such as their value proposition, educational quality, financial stability, and willingness to innovate for example, are obscured or overlooked.

Recently approved federal legislation designed to provide $255 million in financial support to tribal colleges, Hispanic-serving institutions, and HBCUs was hailed in the *Washington Post* as a "Christmas Present" by its chief patron, Senator Lamar Alexander.[23] It is welcome relief to minority-serving institutions so that they can continue to perform their important work. It is a lifeline, but there is no guarantee that it will continue in perpetuity.

If HBCUs are to be saved, ultimately, it is African Americans who will save them for they, better than anyone, know what they have meant to generations of families whose lives were literally transformed by attending one. Alumni and friends of HBCUs must reach deeper into their resources and like the rental car company Avis "try harder" to ensure their sustainability. Homecoming and athletic events return alumni many of whom proudly display expensive Greek letter clothing and paraphernalia, yet some may have given only tepid financial support to their school. Homecoming is special as are sport events and other social and cultural activities that return alumni, friends, and other supporters to campus. In the early to mid-twentieth century many HBCUs created debate teams and choirs, such as the Fisk Jubilee Singers and the Hampton Singers. The Jubilee Singers in one year raised enough money on an international tour to finance the construction of Jubilee Hall, a landmark on Fisk's campus.[24]

In an era when taxpayer support for higher education is at an all-time low, and with fierce competition for students and faculty from well-endowed White colleges and universities, increased HBCU alumni giving is critical. Independent or private HBCUs are particularly vulnerable since many have church or denominational ties. The growth of mega-churches has altered the landscape considerably. HBCUs with Baptist, Episcopal or Methodist ties can no longer depend on denominations for financial support at prior levels because of declining membership. The fervent love for and romanticizing of HBCUs must be matched with financial support if indeed we wish them to have a viable future. A commitment to strengthening enrollment, improving finances, and achieving stable leadership is essential. As much as HBCUs are beloved, there is room for improvement. Spotlighting deficiencies must not be construed as airing dirty linen. Problems can only be resolved when their existence is acknowledged along with a readiness to correct them. Romanticism often gets in the way of meaningful problem-solving and when that occurs it obstructs progress. Also, romanticizing Black colleges obscures the fact that they are not invincible.

Many of the problems HBCUs are experiencing are not new. In fact, many are longstanding. It is not that they defy solution; rather, governing boards and presidents have failed to confront them, preferring to kick the can down the road rather than taking decisive action. Nowhere is this more apparent than in the area of reaffirmation of accreditation. Most HBCUs are located in the Southern states and hold membership in the Commission on Colleges of the Southern Association of Colleges and Universities, commonly referred to as SACS. As member institutions, HBCUs participate in fashioning rules and regulations that each school must follow.

SACS also provides workshops and training for its members to assist with satisfying requirements, yet HBCUs over the past three or four decades have struggled and found themselves on warning or probation. Some have lost accreditation and sued SACS and once having lost, pursue accreditation from another body. Accreditation is absolutely critical to keeping the doors open at HBCUs because most of their students are dependent upon some type of federal loan or financial aid. The loss of accreditation means the loss of federal support. The primary reasons all schools, majority or minority, find themselves in difficult straits are finances, institutional effectiveness, or governance. These conditions did not appear overnight. Rather, HBCU presidents warned of this impending disaster three decades ago in Albert Whiting's, *Guardians of the Flame*. Regrettably, this call to action was routinely ignored.

Unfortunately, too many HBCU presidents today are recruited with the expectation that the first order of business is restoring or reaffirming accreditation. Again, to underscore a point made earlier, accreditation is important because HBCUs enroll a disproportionately high number of students who depend on financial aid, the bulk of which comes from the federal government. Without accreditation, they cannot continue to operate. Accreditation is important but it is essentially a baseline expectation, a floor, and not an aspirational goal in much the same way that one expects a restaurant to have a 100 percent health and sanitation rating by a regulatory health agency.

Black colleges must be competitive and seek to elevate every aspect of their degree offerings. As Benjamin E. Mays, the noted educator and longtime president of Morehouse College, remarked, "Low aim, not failure, is sin." If a school is perennially struggling to achieve and maintain accreditation, it is aiming dangerously low. A tendency to operate on the margins rather than a decisive, strategic approach to scale new heights is a prescription for decline and ultimate failure. This is not what the founders of HBCUs and the countless faculty and staff who labored under difficult conditions for over 150 years envisaged and dedicated their lives and careers for. We must not disparage their hope, dishonor their legacy, and abandon their dreams by failing to aim higher.

Some HBCUs having lost accreditation by SACS have been accepted for membership in the accrediting body Transnational Association of Christian Colleges and Schools, commonly referred to as TRACS. Established in 1979, TRACS fosters "the welfare, interests and development of postsecondary institutions with a Christian purpose and mission." Although a handful of HBCUs have joined TRACS after failing to receive reaffirmation of accreditation by the

Southern Association of Colleges and Universities Commission on Colleges (SACS/COC), it is no panacea for the challenges many of them face regarding enrollment, finances and institutional effectiveness. For some schools leaving SACS for TRACS is tantamount to moving the chairs on the deck of the *Titanic*.

In the matter of finances especially, the critical need to improve the financial condition of HBCUs is seen most vividly in the debt burden of the average HBCU graduate. Presently, that figure is $30,000 and without major intervention it is likely to increase. Of similar concern is the default rate among Black student borrowers which is higher than that of Whites and Latinos. Doug Lederman, of *Inside Higher Ed*, wrote that African American borrowers who completed college had a default rate of 3 percent compared to 55 percent who did not.[25] This is a reflection of the general financial condition many HBCUs find themselves in. Small endowments make it hard to offer scholarships and grants to students who need it most, not only in terms of financial need, but also with regard to academic support that is often needed to compensate for a lack of preparation for college level study.

For decades, White colleges and universities with healthy endowments have successfully recruited Black students with good grades and strong SAT and ACT scores by offering scholarships and grants. This approach has not only resulted in less borrowing by African American students who attend White colleges and universities, but it has led to increased borrowing by African American students enrolled at HBCUs. Consequently, because of their small endowments and limited resources overall, HBCUs find it difficult to compete for students who are well-prepared for college study.

The combined endowments at HBCUs are less than two billion dollars. Harvard's endowment stands at $46 billion. This is illustrative of one of many challenges HBCUs face in the recruitment of students. White universities with sizable endowments are able to use private dollars that subsidize student scholarships. They can also support grants and low interest loans to students, thereby mitigating student debt. Few HBCUs are able to compete in this arena, including some of the most prestigious ones. Billionaire Robert F. Smith's gift of tens of millions of dollars to pay off the debt of Morehouse College graduating seniors in 2019 was of great beneficence, but is it sustainable? Morehouse is one of the most vaunted HBCUs. How did so many students find themselves in the predicament of having to borrow so much money? The public got a glimpse when, less than a year after Smith's widely heralded generosity, the college announced that it was suspending contributions to the employee pension fund. Ensuing protests by faculty and staff caused the school to reverse that decision but its financial problems had been exposed.

The financial challenges faced by the majority of HBCUs, including scholarships to students as well as compensation and benefits for faculty and staff, are all part of a vicious cycle that can only be surmounted by substantial increases to HBCU endowments. Fundraising and achieving solid financial standing should be a high priority for HBCU governing boards and presidents. HBCU alumni also bear responsibility and should step up their support of the institutions that played a huge role in their personal and professional accomplishments.

One of the delightful surprises of 2021 was the unexpected windfall of several multi-million dollar gifts to HBCUs from a number of private sources, the largest of which came from philanthropist MacKenzie Scott. Her unrestricted grants to 22 schools ranged from $4 million to Voorhees College to $50 million to Prairie View A&M University. For each institution this was the largest single gift they had ever received.

Almost immediately several observers began to refer to the gifts as "transformational." While the exuberance is understandable, it is exaggerated. That is because albeit it is true that the funds can be impactful, we also know that money alone will not transform any organization. Rather, a prudent and carefully considered plan must inform and shape funding decisions. This approach is especially warranted in this instance since the funds come with no strings attached. Additionally, the opportunities afforded by this beneficence underscore the need for effective board governance to ensure that these monies will be spent to strengthen and ensure the long-term viability of these iconic institutions.

The financial support of HBCU alumni and other stakeholders is needed now more than ever, because of Covid-19, and its potential to upend life as we know it. This pandemic has caused a huge disruption in higher education, creating not only the need for urgent solutions, but the formulation of a new normal. Education at all levels will change, but especially higher education. Hardest hit will be small colleges and universities, including HBCUs. Most vulnerable are schools that enroll 1000 or fewer students, are located in rural areas, do not have a distinctive market niche, and do not have a large endowment.

Daniel Selingo believes there will be additional long lasting effects. College admissions is one area destined for change as a result of the pandemic. As colleges and universities have switched to online courses, parents and students are looking at the cost-effectiveness of enrolling at boutique schools farther away from home. Instead, some students and their parents are thinking more practically and placing a higher premium on education rather than physical setting, lifestyle and social amenities.[26]

Sweet Briar College in Virginia mirrors the profile above. It was an elite college with a history of serving the needs of privileged young women who could bring their horses with them. It had an endowment of $94 million when the board announced it had decided to close. Alarmed, alumnae all over the country rallied and raised money to keep the doors open. That was an impressive display of philanthropy, but it begs the question of whether Sweet Briar is in fact sustainable.

The United Negro College Fund has 37 member institutions, and while none has an equestrian program like Sweet Briar, all are independent and many have church or denominational ties. Some of these schools may find it difficult, if not impossible, to continue operating. The pandemic exacerbated the condition of schools that were already under-resourced.

When the pandemic hit, several HBCUs had to move to online courses and as was true for majority, or White, schools, some faculty were unprepared for distance learning. Several HBCU students did not have access to the Internet, which meant that online courses were inaccessible. Also, many did not have funds to travel home when campuses were closed. Benedict College in Columbia, South Carolina, relied on its board and the local chapter of The Links to raise money to buy bus and plane tickets, so students could vacate the campus. Wealthy schools with ample endowments could easily fund travel for destitute students, but that was not the case for most colleges and universities, majority- or minority-serving.

The ability of higher education institutions to meet and successfully overcome these challenges rests squarely on the shoulders of governing boards. The pandemic followed decades of challenges at many HBCUs; it also tested their resolve and their ability to survive. Board governance is the Achilles heel of many HBCUs. Now, more than ever, HBCU governing boards must step up.

For alumni and friends of HBCUs this is a watershed moment. Black colleges and universities may be iconic, beloved and praised, but they are not invincible. Since the 1950s, fifteen HBCUs have closed their doors and several have lost accreditation by the Commission on Colleges of the Southern Association of Colleges and Universities (SACS). It will surprise some to learn that at one time there were five Black medical schools. Today there are three, Meharry Medical College, Howard University College of Medicine, and Morehouse School of Medicine, the newest, which opened in 1975.

Long before the pandemic, a number of HBCUs were essentially on life support, flirting with disaster. A number of private or independent HBCUs, often denomination-related, are especially vulnerable due to declining church attendance and the rise of televangelism.

Many of these schools fit the profile for imminent demise: low enrollment, typically less than 1000 students; low endowment; located in a rural area; and without a niche that distinguishes it from other colleges or universities.

In the final analysis, the future of HBCUs turns on effective board governance. Until HBCU boards are more thoughtful and intentional in the recruitment of women and men with the requisite skills and backgrounds for governance, they will continue to flounder. This is only the beginning, however. Once a strong board is in place, the next major responsibility is to select the right person to lead the institution. After the selection of the right leader, boards must be clear about expectations of the president, provide the resources to succeed, hold the president accountable, and get out of the way.

Governing boards must understand and accept the fiduciary duties that are critical to the success of the organization. This is especially important as higher education prepares for a new normal. For fall 2020, analysts predicted a 20 percent decline in enrollment at colleges and universities across the country. For HBCUs, the drop was expected to be higher, possibly as much as 40 percent.

Whether prepared or not, board governance will invariably shape the future of HBCUs just as it does for all higher education institutions. Boards must appreciate the importance of taking the long view. Too often there is a lack of a sense of urgency and an unwillingness to confront harsh realities. Acknowledging problems whether longstanding or new should not be interpreted as airing dirty linen. The only way to fix a problem is to acknowledge its existence.

History seems to move in cycles. Battles seemingly that had been won surface again. Richard Nixon's Southern strategy had worked before. Some observers are convinced that the election of Donald Trump was a direct response to the election of Barack Obama. Some are convinced that today we are revisiting the Post-Reconstruction era. Whatever examples to explain current events one may choose, the simple truth is that what W.E.B. DuBois identified as the problem of the twentieth century, that is, race, persists.

The residuals of the dehumanizing effects of enslavement are deeply embedded in the fabric of American society. We must continue to aggressively eradicate them and there is no better place to begin than education at all levels.

# Postscript

Writing this memoir demanded thoughtful introspection and candor. It also helped that I am a packrat with lots of old papers and documents in my possession. To a degree this was also challenging because rarely do I spend time looking in the rearview mirror. Alas, in this instance it was unavoidable.

If there is a persistent theme throughout my career it is the omnipresence of race. Racism and how to deal with it has been my constant companion. Some feel the sting more deeply than others and the way it is handled is, of course, based on the individual. I have tried to be my authentic self at all times and predictably, the consequences have not always been favorable.

Above all, I am grateful for having been blessed with a loving and supportive family, particularly parents and grandparents, siblings, aunts, uncles and friends. Similarly, I have benefited from a loving and supportive wife and two children; my professional career has been aided significantly by these three exceptional individuals. They, too, have not escaped the effects of race and racism and we have supported each other as we have grappled with our own issues of the moment.

We have tried to help our children understand the realities of race and racism while teaching them never to discriminate against or hate anyone. When our son received his driver's license at age sixteen we had "the talk" about how he should comport himself if he was stopped by a police officer. This is something that White parents don't need to be concerned about. Every Black parent knows that this is a conversation that cannot be avoided.

Race relations have improved a lot since the 1950s and 1960s when I was growing up in the segregated Louisiana. I have witnessed and participated in the election of Black mayors, legislators, a governor and president of the United States. Still, the residual effects of slavery and centuries of racial discrimination although lessened are evident in nearly every aspect of our daily lives. The fact that Black wealth is one-eighth of White wealth is amplified in most social indicators of economic well-being. Education, health and homeownership, for example, shamefully remind us how far we must go to create a more perfect union.

At this stage of my life it is deeply concerning to see overt displays of racism marked by deliberate distortions of history, suppression of information, and willful censorship of what is taught at every level in our schools and universities and what is on the shelves of our libraries. The nation finds itself in a difficult place.

Again, at this stage I thought that as a nation we would have been farther along but we continue to struggle. The election of President Barack Obama was undeniably a milestone given the nation's history. But it was also a double-edged sword. While many saw his election as a sign of progress, others viewed it as evidence of loss of White control. Although demographers had alerted us to the browning of America for decades, the election of a Black man as president underscored its reality and heightened fears. White supremacy reared its ugly head as it has in the past, however; this time it appears more determined than ever to turn back the clock. We dare not let that happen.

The current state of affairs reminds me of two types of feelings I experienced throughout my life as a Black man: (A) You should be happy to be here; and (B) You must constantly prove yourself.

You Should be Happy to Be Here: My academic career was spent at White and historically Black colleges and universities. At White schools I was always made to feel that I had been extended a favor by being hired and surely by being promoted. More often than not I would be taken for granted with assumptions made about my competence or qualifications. If I received a compliment it was usually about my attire but rarely about the quality or accomplishments of my work.

These subtle indicators of racism continue. For example, many universities label offices and titles "Diversity, Equity and Inclusive Excellence." Why "Inclusive Excellence"? Are excellence and inclusiveness incompatible and why should one assume otherwise? One wonders about what type of message this sends about the university and the persons hired.

You Must Constantly Prove Yourself: The second nettlesome source of frustration is always having to prove yourself. Having education, wealth or social standing is never enough. When I've met a White person for the first time usually I have to prove myself all over again. It can be exhausting. I have never forgotten the lesson I taught my son. Whenever I am stopped by a police officer while driving I am careful and cautious lest a wrong move escalate the situation. I expect that at some point my son will have "the talk" with my grandson. That this is a continuing concern in society speaks volumes but it is only one among many.

Presently, our nation's democracy is being tested in ways that it has not since the Civil War. Then, the preponderance of firearms was possessed by the military. Today, many firearms are in the hands of private citizens. Seemingly, the nation has become numbed to mass shootings. The January 6, 2022, assault on the United States Capitol by White supremacists openly brandishing firearms set off alarms still ringing. Our colleges and universities aren't alone in being tested as never before. However, the ways in which they respond to issues related to race can help shape how the nation navigates its current moment of reckoning.

# Chapter Notes

## Chapter One

1. *Martin Luther King, Jr.* (New York: Harper and Row, 1963), 148–149.

## Chapter Two

1. *Lake Charles American Press,* June 10, 1955, 1.
2. Stephen B. Oates, *Let the Trumpet Sound: The Life of Martin Luther King, Jr.* (New York: Harper and Row, 1982), 62.
3. "Coroner Says Body Found in Car Identified," *Lake Charles American Press,* December 1, 1961, 7.

## Chapter Four

1. William H. Grier and Price Cobbs, *Black Rage* (New York: Bantam Books, 1969), 31.

## Chapter Five

1. Ulysses Lee, *The Employment of Negro Troops* (Washington, D.C.: U.S. Government Printing Office, 1965), 10.
2. Benjamin O. Davis, Jr., *Benjamin O. Davis, Jr., American, An Autobiography* (Washington, D.C.: Smithsonian Institution Press, 1991).

## Chapter Six

1. Frank Sherwood, ed., *The Early Years of the Federal Executive Institute* (New York: iUniverse Publishing, 2010), 12.

## Chapter Seven

1. W.L. Holmes, "Chanvellor Schexnider to Leave WSSU for New Job," *Winston-Salem Journal,* November 19, 1999.
2. *Ibid.*
3. *Ibid.*

## Chapter Nine

1. "Job Well Done," *The Daily Press,* May 26, 2011.

## Chapter Ten

1. John Hope Franklin, *Mirror to America* (New York: Farrar, Straus, Giroux, 2005), 4–5.
2. *Ibid.,* 5.
3. *Ibid.,* 167.
4. Marlene L. Daut, "Becoming Full Professor While Black," *Chronicle of Higher Education,* July 28, 2019.
5. Christopher Jencks and David Riesman, "The American Negro College," *Harvard Educational Review* 37, no. 1 (1967): 3–4.

6. *Ibid.*, 59.

7. Statement by Black Graduate Students, Northwestern University, Spring 1971.

8. Patricia A. Matthews, *Written/Unwritten: Diversity and the Hidden Truth of Tenure* (Chapel Hill: University of North Carolina Press, 2016). See also, Daryl G. Smith, *Diversity's Promise for Higher Education*, 2nd ed. (Baltimore: Johns Hopkins University Press, 2015).

9. Clifton R. Wharton, Jr., *Privilege and Prejudice* (East Lansing: Michigan State University Press, 2015), 77.

10. Stefan M. Bradley, "No One Escapes Without Scars," *Chronicle of Higher Education,* April 18, 2019, 14.

11. Michael J. Fortner, "Lifting as We Climb," *Chronicle of Higher Education,* April 18, 2019, 9.

12. Louelle Espinosa, Jonathan Turk, Morgan Taylor, and Hollie Chessman, *Race and Ethnicity in Higher Education: A Status Report* (Washington, D.C.: American Council on Education, 2019), 247.

13. Diyi Li and Cory Koedel, "Representation and Salary Gaps by Race-Ethnicity and Gender at Selective Public Universities," *Educational Researcher* 46, no. 7 (August 2017): 343.

14. Nick Hazelberg, "Little Progress in Diversifying Faculty Ranks," *Inside Higher Ed*, July 2, 2019, 1.

15. Louelle Espinosa, et al., *Race and Ethnicity in Higher Education*, 247.

16. R. Roosevelt Thomas, Jr., "From Affirmative Action to Affirming Diversity," *Harvard Business Review*, March/April 1990, 107–117.

17. *Ibid.*, 107.

18. *Ibid.*, 108.

19. Erin Kelly and Frank Dobbin, "How Affirmative Action Became Diversity Management," *American Behavioral Scientist* 41, no. 7 (April 1998): 960.

20. W.B. Johnson and A.H. Packer, *Workforce 2000: Work and Workers for the Twenty-First Century* (Indianapolis, IN: Hudson Institute, 1987), 9 quoted in Kelly and Dobbins, "How Affirmative Action Became Diversity Management," 974.

21. M.L. Wheeler, "Diversity Training," Conference Board Report Number 1083-94-RR (New York: The Conference Board, 1994) quoted in Kelly and Dobbins, "How Affirmative Action Became Diversity Management," 980.

22. Kelly and Dobbins, "How Affirmative Action Became Diversity Management," 980.

23. Walter Williams, *The Virginian-Pilot*, January 4, 2020, 3.

24. Frederick Douglass, West India Emancipation Speech, delivered at Canandaigua, New York, August 5, 1857.

25. See Daryl G. Smith, *Diversity's Promise for Higher Education* (Baltimore: Johns Hopkins University Press, 2015).

26. *Ibid.*, 110.

27. Diana Ellsworth, Erin Harding, Jonathan Law, and Duwain Pinder, "Racial and Ethnic Equity in U.S. Higher Education," McKinsey & Company, July 18, 2022.

28. Mariappan Jawaharlal, "Why DEI Initiatives Are Likely to Fail," *Inside Higher Ed*, July 21, 2022.

*Chapter Eleven*

1. Camisha L. Jones, "Black Education Association History," Unpublished Paper, 2015, 1.

2. *Ibid.*, 2.

3. AGB Board of Directors, "State-

ment on Justice, Equity and Inclusion," Association of Governing Boards of Universities and College, 2021, Washington, D.C.

## Chapter Twelve

1. Robert A. Nathenson, Andrés Castro Samayoa, and Marybeth Gasman, "Moving Upward and Onward: Income Mobility at Historically Black Colleges and Universities," Rutgers University Center for Minority Serving Institutions, 2019.

2. Franklin, *Mirror to America*, 300.

3. Gabrielle S. Edgcomb, *From Swastika to Jim Crow: Refugee Scholars at Black Colleges* (Malabar, FL: Krieger Publishing, 1993), 78.

4. Rayford W. Logan, *Howard University the First 100 Years, 1867–1967* (New York: New York University Press, 1969), 579.

5. Anne Elizabeth Powell, "The Urgency of Now: HBCUs at a Crossroads," Association of Governing Boards of Universities and Colleges, 2019, 1.

6. *Ibid.*

7. *Ibid.*, 2.

8. Albert N. Whiting, *Guardians of the Flame* (Washington, D.C.: American Association of State Colleges and Universities, 1991), 6.

9. Franklin, *Mirror to America*, 379–380.

10. See also: Richard D. Legon and Alvin J. Schexnider, "Black Colleges Teetering on the Brink Must Chart a New Path," *The Chronicle of Higher Education*, August 4, 2017, and Alvin J. Schexnider, *Saving Black Colleges* (New York: Palgrave Macmillan, 2013).

11. Amatai Etzioni, "Organizational Control and Structure," in *Handbook of Organizations*, edited by James G. March (Chicago: Rand McNally, 1972), 65 (650–677).

12. Stephen R. Covey, *The 7 Habits of Highly Effective People* (New York: Simon & Schuster, 1990), 174.

13. Henry Stoever, "Six Principles of Strategic Leadership," *Trusteeship*, January/February 2020, 7.

14. Alvin J. Schexnider, "Why Board Governance Matters," *Trusteeship*, November/December 2019, 30.

15. Powell, "The Urgency of Now," 2.

16. *Ibid.*

17. Jim Collins, *How the Mighty Fall* (New York: HarperCollins, 2009), 38.

18. Terrance MacTaggart, *The 21st Century Presidency: A Call to Enterprise Leadership* (Washington, D.C.: Association of Governing Boards, 2017), 2.

19. Edgcomb, *From Swastika to Jim Crow*, 58.

20. See: Juan Williams and Duane Ashley, *I'll Find a Way or Make a New One* (New York: HarperCollins, 2004), 144–147.

21. Charles S. Johnson, *The Negro College Graduate* (Chapel Hill: University of North Carolina Press, 1938), 81, quoted in Williams and Ashley, *I'll Find a Way*, 146.

22. *Ibid.*, 145–146.

23. *Washington Post*, December 20, 2019, A10.

24. Williams and Ashley, *I'll Find a Way*, 138.

25. Doug Lederman, *Inside Higher Ed*, December 3, 2019.

26. Frank Bruni, "College Admissions May Never Be the Same," *New York Times*, September 6, 2020, SR3.

# Index

9 781476 693378